# HISTORIC PLACES OF THE AMERICAN REVOLUTION

Attack on Bunker's Hill, With the Burning of Charles Town (detail), unknown artist; National Gallery of Art

"THESE ARE THE TIMES THAT TRY MEN'S SOULS. The summer soldier and the sunshine patriot will, in this crisis, shrink from the service of his country; but he that stands it *now,* deserves the love and thanks of man and woman. Tyranny, like hell, is not easily conquered; yet we have this consolation with us, that the harder the conflict the more glorious the triumph. What we obtain too cheap, we esteem too lightly; 'tis dearness only that gives everything its value. Heaven knows how to put a proper price upon its goods; and it would be strange indeed, if so celestial an article as *Freedom* should not be highly rated."

Thomas Paine
*The American Crisis*
December 23, 1776

National Park Service Guide to the

# HISTORIC PLACES OF THE AMERICAN REVOLUTION

by James V. Murfin

and the Office of Publications staff

**University Press of the Pacific**
**Honolulu, Hawaii**

National Park Service Guide to the Historic Places
of the American Revolution

by
James V. Murfin
National Park Service

ISBN: 1-4102-2110-5

Copyright © 2005 by University Press of the Pacific

Reprinted from the 1974 edition

University Press of the Pacific
Honolulu, Hawaii
http://www.universitypressofthepacific.com

All rights reserved, including the right to reproduce
this book, or portions thereof, in any form.

We prepare now to celebrate a milestone in American history—200 years of vital and enthusiastic life. We cannot do that but by reliving those historic times when a new nation was born in a new world.

From the achievements of heroic men and women who dared all in the name of liberty, we have developed a nation and a way of life dedicated to human freedom and dignity. The strength of their ideas moves us today. We are fortunate that so much of the physical heritage of the American Revolution exists today. The National Park Service is honored to have the responsibility for maintaining many of the most treasured sites of national genesis.

I am proud of how we have carried out that responsibility in preparing the locations so well described in this book for Bicentennial visitors. I invite all readers to enlarge their appreciation of their heritage by visiting these areas. "Being there," you will absorb by the osmosis of your imagination, the strength of a cause that created a nation.

Described in this volume, too, are some 200 other Revolutionary era sites which, while not administered by the National Park Service, can provide many valuable insights into the lives and times of an America two centuries past. In this book and in our many efforts to maintain the national artifacts in our charge we ask you to join us in honoring two hundred years of struggle and progress for mankind.

                                        Ronald H. Walker
                                      Director, National Park Service

# CONTENTS

2 **Historic Places
of the American Revolution**

8 **National, State, and
Local Historic Sites**

Connecticut
Delaware
District of Columbia
Florida
Georgia
Maine
Maryland
Massachusetts
New Hampshire
New Jersey
New York
North Carolina
Pennsylvania
Rhode Island
South Carolina
Vermont
Virginia
West Virginia
The Western Frontier

114 **A Chronology of Political
and Military Events
of the American Revolution**

# HISTORIC PLACES OF THE AMERICAN REVOLUTION

George Washington at Princeton, by Charles Willson Peale, Pennsylvania Academy of Fine Arts, Philadelphia.

At the head of the Green in Lexington, Mass., there is a statue of a minuteman facing the road to Boston, gun in hand as if waiting for the enemy. The man is smaller than you might expect—small for a man who did so much that day in April 1775. The paved highway he faces today bears little resemblance to the dirt country road that ran on past the Green to Concord. Automobiles have replaced the British soldiers, the squeals of children playing have replaced the gunfire, and only monuments now mark the place where Capt. John Parker said "Stand your ground until fired upon." But if there is one place where a person can stand today and say "Here is where it all began," this small patch of ground is it.

Early on the morning of April 19, 1775, Paul Revere raced past the Green and stopped just down the street at a house where John Hancock and John Adams were hiding from the British. Within minutes of his arrival the town bell rang out the alarm, and Parker and his 70-man militia formed two uneven battle lines on the Green. Four and a half hours later the "shot heard round the world" shattered the morning's stillness. "If they mean to have a war," Parker is reported to have said, "let it begin here." The British did not want a war and had no intentions of starting one, but it happened. Two months passed before the American Revolution began in earnest, but the skirmish in this village by a small group of armed Americans marked the beginning of a new era.

This book is an attempt to describe this new era, to note the milestones, to tell what the sites look like today, and to help you step back two centuries into the "presence of the past." These are the places where men and women dreamed of a new world, and where they died to make it a reality. Many of the places are still there to see, to touch, to stand in and to think and perhaps to dream of great people and great events.

Visiting these historic sites can be a satisfying experience, but what you see depends a great deal on what you take with you. Walking along the parapet at Fort Ticonderoga or watching a military demonstration at Saratoga is not quite enough. You are taking an excursion into the past and the true understanding of life two centuries ago will not exist until you are ready to see it. You must be drawn into the magic spell of another time.

Spread across the mountains and valleys of the eastern United States are the battlefields and roads over which two great armies marched, the places they fortified, and the rivers they crossed. Each site played a role in the drama that shaped and molded a loosely knit confederation of colonies into a Nation. Each helped delineate the shape of the dream that became the United States. Standing by a cannon at Yorktown or in Washington's headquarters at Newburgh or in Independence Hall at Philadelphia brings a closer kinship with the people who were there.

This is not a new thought. Some of America's great historians have used historic sites to give their works a special life and authenticity. Writing in the 19th century about the Anglo-French struggle for the North American continent, Francis Parkman sought out the places where it happened. He followed in the footsteps of the armies and absorbed a feeling for the battlefields. He timed his visits and site studies to coincide with the season of the year in which the events occurred. He tried to capture the warmth or chill of the air and the sounds and colors of the woods and landscape. By making the physical environment of his subject a part of his experience Parkman added a new dimension to his histories. In them is a quality, an expression of the drama and meaning of the events that has seldom been duplicated. Benson J. Lossing did this for the Revolutionary War. While much of his *The Pictorial Field-Book of the Revolution* is based on folklore and tradition, he did visit, in the mid-19th century, even the smallest skirmish site and sketched with pen and pencil the many battlefields, monuments, and important buildings. His conversations with the common people who lived on the fields and with the descendants of military figures, coupled with his research into available private papers and public documents, give an invaluable historical perspective to the war.

More recently, Bruce Bliven, Jr. described the British invasion of New York City in his *Battle for Manhattan* with an exciting "you are there" sense of involvement. Details of Gen. Sir William Howe's invasion, and of General Washington's retreat up the island and his stand at Harlem Heights are laid down on a modern day map. Step by step Bliven takes his readers from Kip's Bay at the foot of 34th Street, around Grand Central Station and the United Nations, past Rockefeller Center, and through Central Park to the Columbia University campus, as the British chased the Americans toward what is now 125th Street where they clashed in battle. Despite present-day skyscrapers and traffic-filled streets, Bliven has turned New York City into the farmland and wilderness it once was.

Few have the imagination and genius of a Parkman, the artistic talents of a Lossing, or the patience for detailed research of a

Bliven, but nearly all of us are moved by the great scenes of the past. Visiting them heightens our awareness of our heritage. And, fortunately, there are still places associated with the American Revolution carefully preserved. The people of the United States, acting as individuals, in private groups, and through their local, State, and national governments, have set aside historic sites and buildings or erected memorials where Americans of 200 years ago fought for their independence.

Although Americans revered their heroes—Washington, Jefferson, Allen, Morgan, Gates, Stark, and others—the Nation's first 100 years were not really good times for the preservation of historic sites associated with these people. Independence Hall barely escaped total destruction. It took a proposal to convert Mount Vernon into a hotel to spark public interest in preserving Washington's mansion as a memorial. Important historic houses in Philadelphia were moved to make way for late 19th-century urbanization. The small house in which Jefferson penned the Declaration of Independence was completely demolished. All knowledge of Ethan Allen's burial site was lost long before a monument to this Vermont hero was erected. Important relics, such as cannon captured from the British at the Battle of Bennington and regimental flags and uniforms, were reused in the War of 1812 and lost forever.

The first Revolutionary War historic site to be seriously considered for preservation was the Hasbrouck House, or Washington's Headquarters, at Newburgh, N.Y. This happened almost by default in 1850 when the State acquired the property because of bad debts. The national preservation movement really got underway after the centennial commemoration in 1876 when for the first time, it seems, the American people began to realize the importance of protecting physical evidences of their heritage. Although the movement was slow in starting and even now struggles against modern technology and development pressures, there are a remarkable number of sites and monuments associated with the Revolution that can be visited throughout the eastern States. Some are tucked away on State and county highways, such as the monument to the Battle of Cooch's Bridge near Newark, Del., while others, like Fraunces Tavern in Lower Manhattan, are squeezed between skyscrapers. Still others are located near major thoroughfares, such as Stony Point Battlefield, N.Y. Many of these sites are restored, and the Bicentennial commemoration has focused new attention on their preservation.

Since 1930 the National Park Service has administered and preserved a number of major Revolutionary War historic sites. That year President Herbert Hoover established Colonial National Monument in Virginia (later Colonial National Historical Park). Then in 1933 many battlefields, memorials, and historic sites administered by the War and Agriculture Departments were placed under the jurisdiction of the National Park Service. Prior to this many of the important Revolutionary War sites had been in the hands of private historical societies. For example, the Ford Mansion at Morristown, N.J., where General Washington's headquarters was located during the winter encampments of 1777–78 and 1779–80, had been owned by the Washingon Association of New Jersey since 1873. On March 2, 1933, the National Park Service accepted, in the name of the people of the United States, the mansion, certain property from the town of Morristown, and a valuable collection of Washington memorabilia, all of which now forms the Morristown National Historical Park. These gifts soon led to others. Forty acres of Kings Mountain National Military Park in South Carolina were donated to the National Park Service in 1935 by the Daughters of the American Revolution. This became the nucleus of what is now more than 4,000 acres commemorating that battle of October 7, 1780.

Kings Mountain, along with more than a dozen other battlefields and historic buildings within the National Park System, will play a vital role in the development of the story of the Revolution during the Bicentennial years. This book tries to capture some of the spirit of that period by listing and describing these and other historically significant places of the Revolution. Perhaps by helping you find and visit them it will further serve as a guide to your own Bicentennial commemoration.

# NATIONAL, STATE, AND LOCAL HISTORIC SITES

Minuteman statute on the
Lexington Green, Lexington,
Mass.

Historic sites associated with the American Revolutionary War number in the hundreds. South Carolina alone has 168 skirmish and battle sites, to say nothing of New York and New Jersey through which the British and American armies continuously waged major military campaigns. Thanks to State agencies, patriotic organizations, local historical societies, and county and city governments, students of the American Revolution can visit Jefferson's Monticello, the Boston "Massacre" site, Bunker Hill, Fort Ticonderoga, Brandywine Battlefield, Valley Forge, and the Lexington Green. In most cases the State and local sites are either preserved or excellently restored.

Among Federal agencies, the National Park Service is uniquely charged with the identification, preservation, and interpretation of certain other nationally significant historic sites and monuments associated with the Revolution. Federal Hall, for example, was the meeting place of the Stamp Act Congress in 1765, and, in 1789, the inauguration of George Washington as our first President. Independence Hall in Philadelphia was the scene of the deliberations and decisions of the Second Continental Congress and of the signing of the Declaration of Independence. Minute Man in Massachusetts, Saratoga in New York, and Yorktown in Virginia are, respectively, the sites of the beginning, the turning point, and the end of the military struggle for independence. At Kings Mountain, Cowpens, and Fort Moultrie in South Carolina, Guilford Courthouse and Moores Creek in North Carolina, and Fort Stanwix in New York, occurred significant military engagements, while George Rogers Clark National Historical Park in Vincennes, Ind., represents the western phase of the Revolution. At Morristown, N.J., Washington's army camped during two wartime winters, and at the Vassall-Craigie-Longfellow House in Cambridge, Mass., Washington had his headquarters during the siege of Boston. From Hopewell Village in Pennsylvania came iron for cannon and ammunition to arm the Continental Army. Hopewell and Salem Maritime in Salem, Mass., represent industrial and commercial aspects of the Revolutionary period. John Adams and a succession of distinguished Adamses are represented at Adams National Historic Site, Quincy, Mass. Hamilton Grange in New York City was the home of Alexander Hamilton, who first gained fame as a young revolutionary pamphleteer and artillery officer. And George Washington is represented by a reconstruction of his birthplace at Wakefield in Virginia. Together, these units of the National Park Service represent major phases of the Revolutionary story.

Many National Park Service (NPS) areas have periodical "Living History" demonstrations. At the Revolutionary War sites these include the firing of flint-lock rifles and period cannon, and demonstrations of military camp life and domestic crafts. Such programs involve NPS personnel and volunteers in uniform and costume. The description of each NPS site included in this book, where applicable, indicates the kind of program you can see.

The National Park Service welcomes handicapped persons. Provisions for persons using wheelchairs and certain other patients have been made, where possible, and the park staff will help make your visit as pleasant as possible.

Many of the places identified in this book are National Historic Landmarks. This official recognition indicates that the site, publicly or privately owned, is a special part of America's heritage, judged by the Secretary of the Interior and the National Park Service to possess significance for all Americans and to be worthy of a place on the National Register of Historic Places. Landmark designation calls public attention to historic places judged to have exceptional value to the Nation as a whole rather than to a particular State or locality. This program recognizes and encourages the preservation efforts of State, local, and private agencies and groups. It encourages the owners of Landmark properties to observe simple preservation precepts. And it offers the technical advice and assistance of Federal preservation experts in attaining this end.

Here, grouped by State, are some of the more significant historic places associated with the American Revolution. National Historic Landmarks are indicated by the initials NHL. Some structures, though National Historic Landmarks, are private property and not open to the public. Such sites are indicated "private." Site and city location numbers correspond to numbers on individual State maps.

Although Connecticut's jagged shoreline was the object of British naval attacks and numerous raids on supply centers, no major battles took place on her soil during the Revolution. Other than the forts at Groton, which were attacked by a naval force under the command of American defector Benedict Arnold, the colony has only a few significant Revolutionary War sites. The colony is best represented in the Revolution by the legendary Israel Putnam, already an American hero when the Revolution began.

## Connecticut

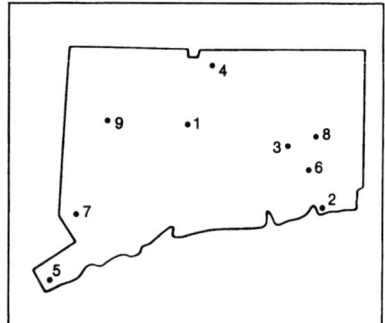

Count de Rochambeau, French commander who met with Washington at the Webb House; a French engraving from a life portrait.

**Connecticut contributed the second largest number of troops to the war: 9,000 militia, 31,939 in the Continental Army. And all three of the Purple Hearts awarded by George Washington went to Connecticut men.**

Joseph Webb House, Wethersfield

Jonathan Trumbull War Office. Lebanon.

Conference Room at the Webb House, Wethersfield.

Governor Jonathan Trumbull House. Lebanon.

Oliver Wolcott and Samuel Huntington, Connecticut signers of the Declaration of Independence.

Regimental flag of the Connecticut 2nd Light Dragoons; Connecticut State Library Museum, Hartford

Gen. Israel Putnam, from a sketch by Benson J. Lossing.

By the spring of 1781 a war weariness had settled over colonial America. Action in the North was stalemated and most of the Continental Army was in the South. General Washington's command in and around West Point was inactive. It was becoming increasingly obvious that a combined allied offensive must be undertaken if the American cause was not to languish. On May 22, the American and French commanders met at the Connecticut town of Wethersfield [1]. This meeting resulted in the joint Franco-American campaign that led ultimately to victory at Yorktown. The Count de Rochambeau and General Washington met that day in "the house of Joseph Webb, Esq.," built in 1752 and occupied by Webb's widow. Today the **Joseph Webb House,** 211 Main St., is operated by the Society of Colonial Dames as a museum. This National Historic Landmark is a splendid example of 18th-century architecture and furnishings.

Other Connecticut sites associated with the Revolution are **Fort Griswold,** Groton [2], subject of a naval attack by Benedict Arnold in 1781; **Governor Jonathan Trumbull House** (NHL), Lebanon [3], birthplace of John Trumbull, artist of the Revolution, and home of the wartime governor of Connecticut; **Jonathan Trumbull War Office,** Lebanon [3], from which Governor Trumbull arranged supplies for the Continental Army; **Old Newgate Prison** (NHL), East Granby [4], where British prisoners of war were held; **Putnam Cottage,** Greenwich [5], originally Knapp's Tavern, where Gen. Israel Putnam was supposedly staying in 1779 when surprised by the British; **Silas Deane House** (NHL), Wethersfield [1], home of America's first envoy to France during the Revolution; **General Jedediah Huntington House** (private), Norwichtown [6]; **Putnam Memorial State Park,** Redding [7], site of the 1778–79 winter encampment of Continental troops under Gen. Israel Putnam; and three houses associated with Connecticut's signers of the Declaration of Independence: **Samuel Huntington Birthplace** (private, NHL), Scotland [8]; **William Williams House** (private, NHL), Lebanon [3]; and **Oliver Wolcott House** (private, NHL), Litchfield [9].

Connecticut travel, historic sites, and Bicentennial information can be obtained by writing to:

Connecticut Development Commission, 210 Washington St., Hartford, CT 06106.

Connecticut American Revolution Bicentennial Commission, 59 South Prospect St., Hartford. CT 06106.

Delaware, the first colony to ratify the Constitution and thus the first State, claims only one military skirmish, the Battle at Cooch's Bridge, a small encounter between Howe's and Washington's troops during the British advance on Philadelphia. Delaware, however, made a significant contribution of troops to the war effort: 1,000 militia, 2,386 Continental Army.

## Delaware

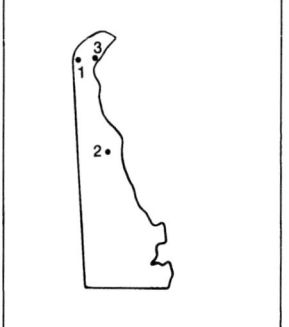

John Dickinson House, Dover.

Delaware Troops Leaving the Dover Green, 1777, by Stanley M Arthurs; Old State House, Dover.

Monument to the Battle of Cooch's Bridge, near Newark.

Old Court House, New Castle.

Caesar Rodney, Delaware signer of the Declaration of Independence; Statuary Hall, U.S. Capitol, Washington, D.C.

On September 3, 1777, about 700 American troops under Gen. William Maxwell ambushed a part of Sir William Howe's British Army advancing against Philadelphia at a little bridge over Christiana Creek, two miles southeast of Newark. The redcoats gradually forced the Continentals back and, when Maxwell's units became disorganized, the men fled to rejoin the main army. The **Battle of Cooch's Bridge** was over in minutes and had no effect on the British campaign. The **Cooch House,** built in 1760, still stands near the bridge, one mile east of Del. 896 in New Castle County [1], and is privately owned. Cornwallis occupied this house during his army's advance from Head-of-Elk, Md., to Philadelphia. A monument near the Cooch House grounds commemorates the battle.

Thomas Jefferson said that John Dickinson, known as the Penman of the Revolution, "will be consecrated in history as one of the great worthies of the Revolution." Indeed, one writer has said, "In the literature of that struggle, his position is as pre-eminent as Washington in war, Franklin in diplomacy, and Morris in finance." Dickinson's *Letters of a Farmer in Pennsylvania to the Inhabitants of the British Colonies* had great influence on Revolutionary thinking. He headed the conservative faction that opposed both British colonial policy and the radicals' drive for independence. The restored **John Dickinson House** (NHL) near Dover [2] is the surviving structure most intimately associated with him. The house is owned by the State of Delaware.

Other Delaware sites associated with the Revolution are the **Old Court House** (NHL), New Castle [3], seat of the colonial and revolutionary governments to 1777; and **Old State House,** New Castle [3], seat of the revolutionary government after 1777.

Delaware travel, historic sites, and Bicentennial information can be obtained by writing to:

Bureau of Travel Development, Department of Community Affairs and Economic Development, The Green, Dover, DE 19901.

Delaware American Revolution Bicentennial Commission, P.O. Box 2476, Wilmington, DE 19899.

The District of Columbia did not exist at the time of the Revolution, but today it is a veritable storehouse of art and artifacts associated with the events and personalities of the war, many of which are displayed in the Museum of History and Technology, Smithsonian Institution.

## District of Columbia

Signers of the Declaration of Independence.

The gunboat *Philadelphia*; Smithsonian Institution.

Bow of the *Philadelphia* showing the 24-pound British shot which sank the gunboat; Smithsonian Institution.

The Museum of History and Technology on Constitution Avenue, houses one of the finest collections of artifacts of the Revolution: Washington's uniform and other personal military equipment, including one of several tents he used in the field; weapons, swords, and paintings; and the only surviving gunboat built and manned by American forces during the war. The gondola *Philadelphia* (NHL) was one of 15 small craft with which Benedict Arnold fought Sir Guy Carleton's British fleet in the battle off Valcour Island, Lake Champlain, on October 11, 1776. In 1935 the *Philadelphia*, remarkably well preserved by the cold waters of the lake, was salvaged from the midchannel of Valcour Bay. After raising her guns, a 12-pounder and two 9-pounders, the hull was lifted 57 feet to the surface and towed to the beach. Besides her guns, the vessel contained hundreds of other relics, including shot, cooking utensils, tools, buttons, buckles, and human bones. The gunboat was exhibited at various places on Lake Champlain and the Hudson River before being placed on display at the Smithsonian Institution in 1960.

This Nation's three most precious documents emanating from the Revolutionary War period—the **Declaration of Independence,** the **Constitution,** and the **Bill of Rights,** the documents that established the United States and upon which all laws of the land are based—are on public view in the main hall of the National Archives.

Throughout the city of Washington there are many statues and monuments commemorating men of the Revolution including **Com. John Barry, Gen. Nathanael Greene, Nathan Hale, Thomas Jefferson, Com. John Paul Jones, Gen. Thaddeus Kosciuszko, Gen. Lafayette, Count Casimir Pulaski, Count Jean Baptiste Rochambeau, Gen. Frederick Von Steuben, Gen. Artemus Ward,** and **George Washington.** And there is the magnificent Federal City itself, named for the Commander in Chief of the Continental Army and first President of the United States, and designed by Pierre Charles L'Enfant, an engineering officer in the Revolution.

Washington, D.C., travel, historic sites, and Bicentennial information can be obtained by writing to:

National Capital Parks, National Park Service, 1100 Ohio Dr., SW, Washington, DC 20242.

Bicentennial Commission of the District of Columbia, 1407 L St., NW, Washington, DC 20005.

In 1763, as a result of the French and Indian War, Spain ceded Florida to Great Britain. British forces garrisoned and strengthened Castillo de San Marcos at St. Augustine on the east coast. Though the western part of the colony was more inhabitable, and thus more prosperous, East Florida became a military base for the British southern campaigns in the Revolution. Late in the war at Pensacola a dramatic battle between Spanish and British forces brought an end to British military power in Florida.

## Florida

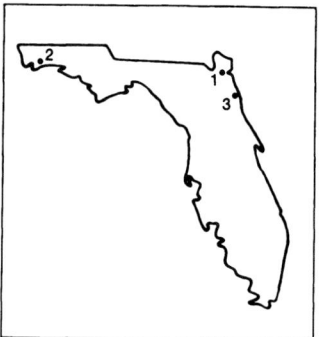

Castillo de San Marcos, St. Augustine, used as a prison for patriots

Castillo de San Marcos.

Three South Carolina signers of the Declaration of Independence imprisoned at Castillo de San Marcos: Arthur Middleton, above, Edward Rutledge, top right, and Thomas Heyward, bottom right

While the Thirteen Colonies joined against George III, Florida re-remained loyal to the King. As Philadelphia patriots declared their independence, St. Augustine Loyalists burned effigies of John Hancock and Samuel Adams. For a while East Florida became an armed camp; soldiers, supplies, and equipment flooded the small ports, and hundreds of Loyalist refugees from the war-torn colonies settled in and around the former Spanish fortifications.

The **Castillo de San Marcos** was the main military base. From here British troops marched against Savannah and Charleston and rangers made raids into the Georgia country.

Though Spanish spies furnished the Americans details of the coastal defenses and drafted plans for the capture of the Castillo, little resulted but additional British guns and reinforced palisades and earthworks. American forces from Georgia made three unsuccessful attempts against St. Augustine between 1776 and 1778. The second and principal confrontation took place north of Jacksonville [1], where Int. 95 crosses the Nassau River. The battle at Thomas Creek, May 17, 1777, was poorly conceived, poorly coordinated, and poorly executed and involved only about 200 men on each side. British regulars and their Indian allies defeated the Americans and essentially relieved St. Augustine of any military danger. The **Thomas Creek Battlefield** is owned by the State and survives relatively unchanged.

St. Augustine became known chiefly as a prisoner-of-war camp during the Revolution, beginning as early as 1776 when men taken in Governor Dunmore's early Virginia campaigns were transported there. As many as 300 French and Spanish seamen and American patriots were imprisoned at the Castillo, not the least of whom were three of South Carolina's four signers of the Declaration of Independence: Arthur Middleton, Edward Rutledge, and Thomas Heyward.

By special permission, on July 4, 1781, all three signers dined together in one of the most unique celebrations of American independence ever. As the patriots enjoyed their brief moment together in a cell, they were served an English plum pudding with a tiny "Stars and Stripes" flag on top. Together, to the tune of "God Save the King," they sang "God save the thirteen States, Thirteen United States, God save them all."

Though the Americans had long sought a means of reducing British influence in West Florida, and indeed had made a feeble attempt in 1778 to do so, it was left to the Spanish to threaten the center of British power at Fort George at Pensacola. Spain had allied itself with France and in June 1779 declared war against Great Britain. In August of that year, under the leadership of Bernardo de Galvez, Governor of Louisiana, Spanish forces captured the British outposts on the lower Mississippi River.

In the early spring of 1781, Galvez, the last great Spanish military figure serving his country in the New World, led a month-long siege of Fort George. In a brilliant and gallant naval maneuver Galvez landed more than 7,000 troops on March 9. On April 28 the Spaniards broke through the outer fortifications and on May 8 succeeded in dropping a shell on the powder magazine. The explosion killed or disabled over 100 of the 900 British defenders and demolished one of the principal redoubts. The main assault in what has been called the **Battle of Pensacola** brought the fort's capitulation the following day. Florida was once more in the hands of the Spanish. The Treaty of Paris officially gave Florida to Spain in 1783. In 1821 it was ceded to the United States.

The site of Fort George is located on Palafox Hill (once Gage's Hill), adjacent to Lee Square overlooking the Pensacola business district [2]. No archeological diggings have been made and only a State historical marker designates the site of this little-known but dramatic battle of the American Revolution.

**Castillo de San Marcos National Monument** is today administered by the National Park Service and is located at St. Augustine [3]. Although interpretation is keyed to the pre-Revolutionary Spanish period, the American Revolution Bicentennial Commission of Florida has selected Castillo de San Marcos as a Florida Bicentennial Trail site.

Florida travel, historic sites, National Park Service, and Bicentennial information can be obtained by writing to:

Visitor Inquiry, Department of Commerce, Collins Building, Tallahassee, FL 32304.

Castillo de San Marcos and Fort Matanzas National Monuments, 1 Castillo Dr., St. Augustine, FL 32084.

The American Revolution Bicentennial Commission of Florida, The Capitol, Tallahassee, FL 32304.

Long before Sherman's march through Georgia during the Civil War (1861–65), the British had a march of their own—across the colony from the coast to Augusta following the capture of Savannah. The British campaign in Georgia has been considered of little military importance, but it was a brutal occupation that left countless dead, both military and civilian. Like other southern colonies, Georgia had greater numbers in the State militia than in the Continental Army: 8,000 militia, 2,679 army.

## Georgia

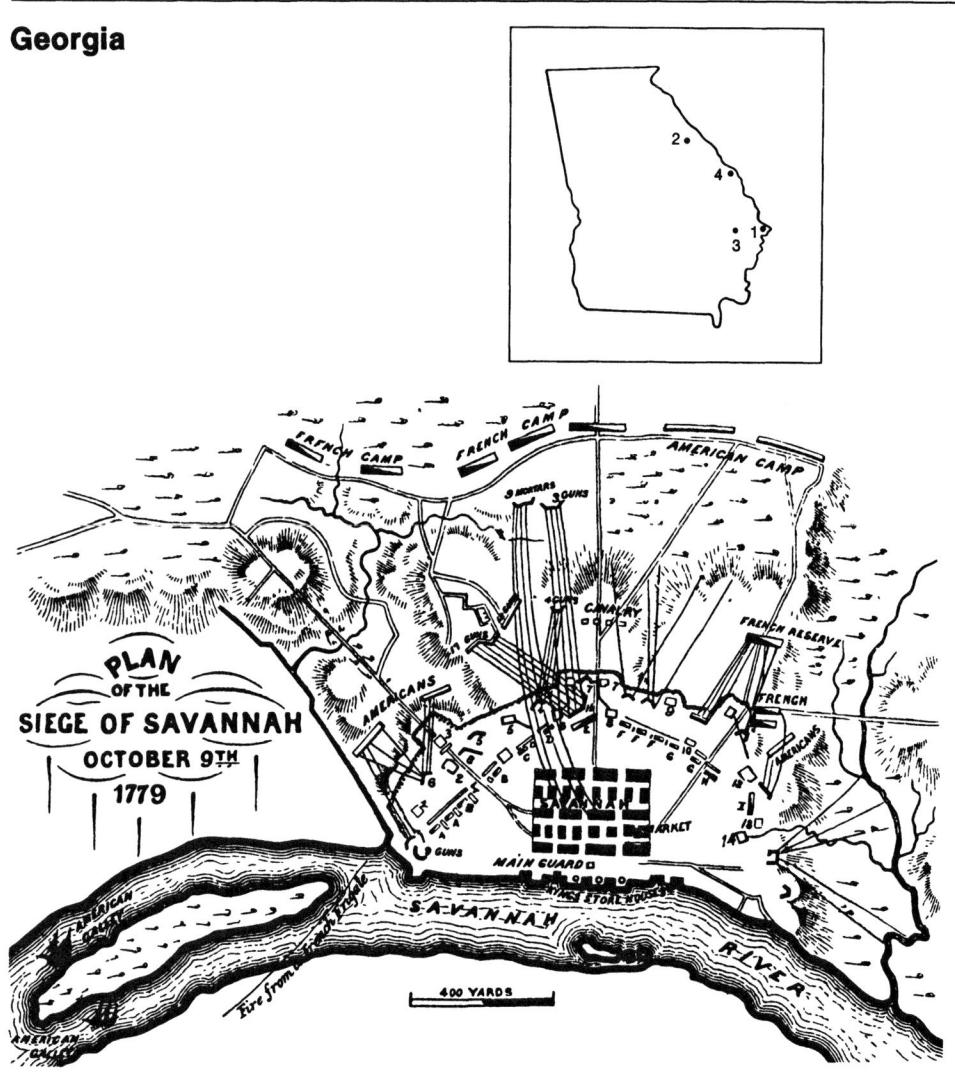

On December 29, 1778, Lt. Col. Archibald Campbell took the river port of **Savannah** [1] with 3,500 British troops. Eighty-three Americans died and 453 were captured as the war turned to the South, and Savannah became an occupied city until the end of the war. A combined French-American force unsuccessfully besieged the city from September 3 to October 26, 1779. The British evacuated Savannah July 11, 1782.

On the morning of February 14, 1779, Georgia and South Carolina militia under Andrew Pickens surprised a Tory force under Col. John Boyd about 8 miles southwest of Washington, Ga. The Tories recovered and made a momentary advance, but they were driven back across Kettle Creek. When Boyd fell mortally wounded, the Tories dispersed. The small **Battle of Kettle Creek** temporarily stopped the occupation of Augusta, but it had no decisive effect on the war in general except to check the Loyalist cause in Georgia and South Carolina and boost patriot morale. Twelve acres of the battlefield have been preserved by the Daughters of the American Revolution, and it appears today very much as it did at the time of the battle. The site is located 8 miles southwest of Washington via Ga. 44 [2].

Other Georgia sites associated with the Revolution are **Fort Morris,** Midway [3], garrisoned fortification on Midway River but not involved in any major engagement; **McKay House,** Augusta [4], British-Indian trading post, scene of several important attacks by Georgia patriots; **Spring Hill Redoubt,** Savannah [1], a key British position on October 9, 1779, in the climax of the siege of Savannah; and two homes associated with George Walton, a Georgia signer of the Declaration of Independence, **College Hill** (private, NHL), and **Meadow Gardens,** Augusta [4].

Georgia travel, historic sites, and Bicentennial information can be obtained by writing to:

Tourist Division, Georgia Department of Community Development, P.O. Box 38097, Atlanta, GA 30334.

Georgia Commission, National Bicentennial Celebration, Suite 520, South Wing, 1776 Peachtree St., NW, Atlanta, GA 30309.

**Maine, then a part of the Massachusetts Bay Colony, suffered numerous British naval attacks, but the most significant military event in the colony was Benedict Arnold's expedition to Quebec.**

## Maine

Fort Western, Augusta, where Arnold's expedition to Quebec began.

Great Falls of the Chaudiere River in Canada, one of Arnold's many obstacles.

Sir Guy Carleton, commander of British forces at Quebec opposing Arnold's attack, by M. B. Messer; Public Archives of Canada, Ottawa.

Arnold's March to Quebec,
by N.C. Wyeth.

Carrying-place Stream, the beginning of Arnold's overland route in northern Maine.

Benedict Arnold, from a sketch by Benson J. Lossing.

Under orders from George Washington, Benedict Arnold began his march to Quebec at **Fort Western** (Augusta) [1] on September 24, 1775. Moving up the **Kennebec River** [2] about 70 miles, he portaged to the **Dead River** [3], followed the Dead River to **Chain of Ponds** [4] near the present Canadian border, and arrived at **Quebec** in early November with 600 of his original 1,100 men. Although Arnold failed in his objective of capturing the city, the epic journey forced Howe to divide his army to provide reinforcements for Canada. **Arnold's Route** can be followed with considerable accuracy today. Many of the campsites and portages are marked by the State of Maine and the Arnold Expedition Historical Society.

The earthworks at **Fort George** in Castine [5], built and occupied by the British in 1779, have been preserved. The blockhouses at **Fort Halifax** (NHL), Winslow [6], and **Fort Western,** Augusta [1], have been reconstructed.

Another Maine site associated with the Revolution is **Montpelier,** Thomaston [7], a reconstruction of Gen. Henry Knox's home in the later years of his life.

Maine travel, historic sites, and Bicentennial information can be obtained by writing to:

Maine Department of Economic Development, State Office Building, Augusta, ME 04330.

Maine State American Revolution Bicentennial Commission, State House, Augusta, ME 04330.

**Although Maryland saw no military action during the Revolution, its Maryland Line fought in almost every major engagement and was among the elite of the Continental Army. The colony contributed 9,000 militia, 13,912 army. Maryland's distinguished citizens included Charles Carroll of Carrollton and Gen. William Smallwood. It was in the Maryland State House at Annapolis that the Continental Congress met when the Treaty of Paris was ratified.**

## Maryland

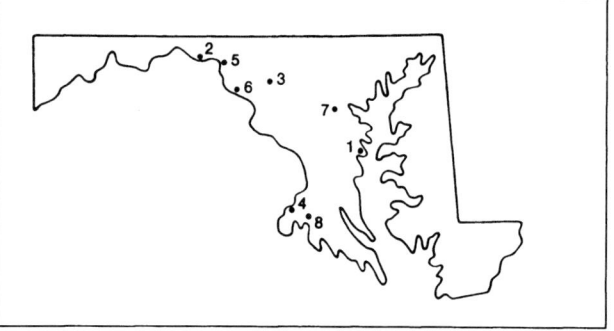

| | | |
|---|---|---|
| Habre d'Venture, Port Tobacco | Smallwood's Retreat, Mason Springs. | State House, Annapolis. Paca House, Annapolis. |

John Paul Jones, from an early engraving.

Old Senate Chamber, State House, Annapolis.

Annapolis waterfront.

Flag of Pulaski's Legion, from a sketch by Benson J. Lossing; displayed at the Maryland Historical Society, Baltimore.

First Maryland Regiment at Fort Frederick.

Fort Frederick State Park.

For 9 months the **Maryland State House** (NHL) in Annapolis [1] was the seat of the Continental Congress. Here in December 1783 the Congress received Washington's resignation as commander in chief of the Continental Army and in January 1784 ratified the Treaty of Paris that ended the war. Built in 1722, this brick structure is the oldest statehouse still in use; expanded, it now houses the offices of the governor and the State legislature. The old **Senate Chamber,** where the historic events took place, has been restored. **Fort Frederick,** located 5 miles south of Clear Spring [2] in western Maryland, off U.S. 40 and Int. 70, was built in 1756 as one of a chain of posts guarding frontier settlements from Indian attacks. During the Revolution the fort held British prisoners captured at Saratoga and Yorktown. An excellent fort reconstruction is part of **Fort Frederick State Park** where periodic demonstrations are presented by the reactivated First Maryland Regiment.

Other Maryland sites associated with the Revolution are the **Hessian Barracks,** Frederick [3], one of two buildings used as a prisoner-of-war camp; **Smallwood's Retreat,** Mason Springs [4], the reconstructed home of Gen. William Smallwood, commander of Maryland troops during the Revolution; **John Paul Jones Tomb,** U.S. Naval Academy Chapel (NHL), Annapolis [1]; **Springfield,** Gen. Otho Holland Williams House (private), Williamsport [5]; **Rose Hill Manor,** home of wartime Governor Thomas Johnson, Frederick [3]; **Needwood,** Gov. Thomas Sim Lee House (private), Knoxville [6]; **Peggy Stewart House,** Annapolis [1], onetime home of Thomas Stone, signer of the Declaration of Independence, St. Thomas Jenifer, signer of the Constitution, and the owner of the *Peggy Stewart,* mechant ship involved in Maryland's "Tea Party" in October 1774; and three houses associated with Maryland's signers of the Declaration of Independence: **Doughoregan Manor** (private, NHL), near Ellicott City [7], home of Charles Carroll of Carrollton, last survivor of the signers; **Habre-de-Venture** (private, NHL), Port Tobacco [8], home and grave site of Thomas Stone; and **William Paca House** (NHL), Annapolis [1].

Maryland travel, historic sites, and Bicentennial information can be obtained by writing to:

Division of Tourism, Department of Economic and Community Development, 2525 Riva Road, Annapolis, MD 21401.

Maryland Bicentennial Commission, Department of Economic and Community Development, 2525 Riva Road, Annapolis, MD 21401.

This is where it all began. Except for Virginia, Massachusetts is the colony in which the loudest voices against British policies were raised. Open agitation, overt acts of resistance, and the manipulation of public opinion against British officials were everyday occurrences in Massachusetts after British troops were stationed in Boston in 1768. The Boston "Massacre," the "Boston Tea Party," and the levying of the Boston Port Bill were among the incidents on both sides that brought about the eventual

## Massachusetts

Minuteman Statue, North Bridge, Concord.

clash of arms at Lexington and Concord in 1775. Although first blood was shed here, the tide of war soon shifted to neighboring colonies. Massachusetts had the largest number of troops in the war: 20,000 militia, 67,907 Continental Army.

North Bridge, Minute Man National Historical Park, Concord.

The famous Doolittle drawings of the action on April 19, 1775: The Battle of Lexington; A View of the Town of Concord; The Engagement at the North Bridge in Concord; A View of the South Part of Lexington.

William Dawes, from an original by Gullagher, Cary Memorial Library, Lexington

Derby House, Salem.

Buckman Tavern, Lexington.

Bunker Hill Monument, Charlestown.

Equestrian statue of Paul Revere, with Old North Church in the background, Boston.

Historic site preservation in Boston has been remarkable in that so many sites have survived neglect and redevelopment over the years. Boston [1] had to reconstruct very little. Although most of the sites are sandwiched between modern office buildings and freeways, they retain a certain historical flavor. The site of the "Boston Tea Party" was filled in many years ago and now only a plaque many yards away marks this historic event, but the graves of Hancock, Adams, and Revere are there lying peacefully between buildings in the business district; and across the river at Charlestown only the crest of Breed's Hill rises above row after row of residences. All of these sites are a part of Boston's heritage and all are marked in some way. The Freedom Trail, beginning with the Common and ending at Old North Church, is a 1½-mile walking tour of the old section of town, marked with red brick embedded in the sidewalks and streets. The tour takes about 3 hours.

The **Common (Stop 1)** is one of the oldest parks in the country, originally set aside in 1634 for common use as a "cow pasture and training field." Here the British assembled before the Battle of Bunker Hill. From the Charles Street side of the Common, near the Central Burial Ground, the British embarked on their march to Lexington on April 18, 1775. And in the cemetery is buried colonial painter Gilbert Stuart. **Stop 2** on the Freedom Trail is the **State House** (NHL) on Beacon Hill. Although it does not date to the Revolution, it does contain a number of priceless Revolutionary War relics. The **Park Street Church (Stop 3)** is early 19th-century, but nearby is **Stop 4,** the **Old Granary Burying Ground** where Samuel Adams, John Hancock, Paul Revere, and victims of the Boston "Massacre" are buried. The cemetery takes its name from the Town Granary that once stood on the site of the Park Street Church and was part of the Common. **Stop 5** is **King's Chapel** (NHL), Tremont and School Streets, erected in 1754 on the site of the original 1686 church. William Dawes, the "other man" who rode to Lexington and Concord to warn of the British approach on the night of April 18, 1775, is buried in the churchyard.

The Freedom Trail leads past the site of the **First Public School (Stop 6),** the statue of **Benjamin Franklin (Stop 7),** and the **Old Corner Book Store (Stop 8),** to the **Old South Meeting House** (NHL) **(Stop 9)** at Washington and Milk Streets, where the **"Boston Tea Party"** originated. In this Congregational church on the night of December 16, 1773, several thousand citizens sat into the night waiting for word that Gov. Thomas Hutchinson had placed a ban on the shiploads of tea waiting in the harbor. When he refused, the crowd, some dressed as Indians, rushed to Griffins Wharf, now along Atlantic Avenue near the Fort Point Channel, boarded the ships and threw the chests of tea into the harbor. Very near the church is **Stop 10,** the birthplace of Benjamin Franklin, whose parents are buried in the Old Granary Burying Ground.

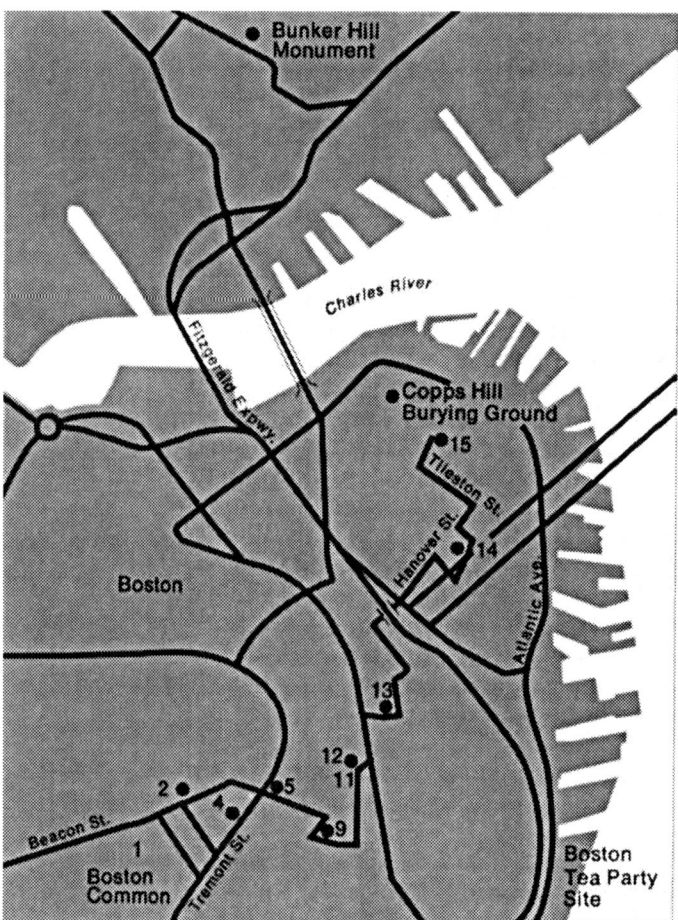

The **Old State House** (NHL), **(Stop 11),** Washington Street at the head of State Street, was erected in 1713. Here in the legislative chambers on February 24, 1761, James Otis argued against the

Writs of Assistance designed to end widespread smuggling of contraband goods. It was this speech that inspired John Adams to say: "Then and there the child independence was born."
In the square in front of the Old State House, on the evening of March 5, 1770, the Boston "Massacre" occurred. This event is commemorated by a large metal disk in the street at State and Congress Streets **(Stop 12)**.

**Faneuil Hall** (NHL), **(Stop 13),** called the "Cradle of Liberty," served as a market place, townhall, and meetinghouse during the Revolutionary movement. It now contains some very fine Revolutionary paintings, a library, and a military museum. Along its street level are open markets operated much the same as in colonial times.

The Freedom Trail follows Stone and Hanover Streets underneath the Fitzgerald Expressway to the **Paul Revere House** (NHL) **(Stop 14),** at 19-21 North Square. Built in 1670, this is the oldest frame house in Boston. Paul Revere purchased it in 1770, and it was from here that he set out on his famous ride.

The British expedition that marched out of Boston on the night of April 18, 1775, had a specific mission: seek out any military stores they suspected were being hidden in Concord and find radical leaders John Hancock and Samuel Adams. Suspecting the British intentions, the patriots set up an alarm system whereby the minutemen could be warned of approaching danger. From the belfry of Old North Church two lanterns signaled the patriots that the British were loading boats to move across the Charles River. Paul Revere and William Dawes rode out to pass the word. **Old North Church** (NHL) still stands at 189 Salem Street **(Stop 15)**, and one of the two lanterns can be seen at the Antiquarian Society in Concord. Maj. John Pitcairn, the British second in command on the march to Lexington, who was later killed at Bunker Hill, lies buried in the crypt beneath Old North Church. The Freedom Trail ends at this point.

On the Lexington Green (NHL) [2] on the morning of April 19, 1775, British forces from Boston seeking hidden military stores met a group of minutemen, a small band of 60 or 70 armed farmers who had been alerted by Paul Revere. The British were ordered not to fire first. Sensing the hopelessness of the situation, Capt. John Parker, commanding the Americans, ordered his men to disperse. Then "the shot heard 'round the world" rang out.

Fired by whom no one knows, but the first blood had been drawn. Eight Americans lay dead and ten more were wounded.

Though a major battle would not occur for another 2 months, the British faced armed rebellion. The Lexington Green, lined with lovely colonial homes, is one of America's most famous landmarks. On the east side of the common facing the road by which the British approached, Henry H. Kitson's statue of a minuteman stands on a pile of rocks over a stone fountain. The historic Revolutionary Monument, erected in 1799 to commemorate the eight minutemen killed here, occupies the southwest corner of the Green, and behind it is a tomb to which the remains of the dead were moved from the old burying ground in 1835. Two inscribed boulders have also been placed on the Green. One identifies the site of the old belfry, from which rang out the alarm to the minutemen. The other, near the northwest corner, marks one flank of Captain Parker's line. It bears, in addition to designs of musket and powder horn, the words Parker is alleged to have said: "Stand your ground. Don't fire unless fired upon. But if they mean to have a war, let it begin here."

Near the Green is **Buckman Tavern** (NHL), the oldest of Lexington's hostelries. The proprietor, John Buckman, was a member of the Lexington company of minutemen, and his public house was a convenient gathering place for his comrades on drill days. Here is where they met during the evening and throughout the night preceding the arrival of British troops on April 19, 1775. The **Hancock-Clarke House** (NHL), a few doors away on Hancock Street, is where John Adams and John Hancock were staying on the night of April 18, 1775, when Paul Revere warned them to take cover from the British. Now owned by the Lexington Historical Society, the house exhibits many Lexington artifacts.

While minutemen assembled at Buckman Tavern in Lexington, 6 miles to the west, in **Concord** [3], a similar group of armed citizens met at **Wright's Tavern** (NHL) to consider what action they would take against the oncoming British troops. With the public meetinghouse on one side and the militia training ground on the other, Wright's Tavern was a favorite spot for Concord's business meetings and friendly gatherings, and thus played an important role in the transaction of the town's civil and military affairs.

The news of the impending clash arrived in Concord about 2 a.m., and by 7 a.m., when the British column appeared, nearly 400 minutemen and militia had been deployed at strategic locations. They met at the North Bridge in a battle that lasted about 3 minutes. When the smoke cleared, two Americans lay dead and four wounded. Three British soldiers were killed and nine wounded.

By mid-morning the British began their retreat to Boston, a 16-mile march that was every bit as deadly as the fights at Lexington and Concord. By nightfall the British had lost 19 officers and 250 men killed and wounded. The Americans had lost about 90 killed and wounded and 5 missing.

Politically, the day at Lexington and Concord had been just what the American agitators had needed to mobilize popular support for their cause against England. This somewhat insignificant military victory was turned into a major event in world history, and the sites became hallowed ground.

Both small towns and the battle road between them have resisted modern intrusions to some extent. The North Bridge at Concord has been reconstructed and monuments dot the landscape. Through the efforts of the community, much of the colonial flavor remains.

**Minute Man National Historical Park,** established in 1959, contains three units: the Lexington-Concord Battle Road, a 4-mile corridor along the historic battle road and Mass. 2A westward from Meriam's Corner; **Old North Bridge** in Concord; and **Wayside,** home of the Alcotts, Nathaniel Hawthorne, and Margaret Sidney, on the Lexington Road (Mass. 2A) in Concord.

The Fiske Hill information station is on Mass. 2A, just west of Mass. 128. One mile west on Mass. 2A is the park headquarters with year-round information services. An interpretive station is in the Buttrick Mansion overlooking the North Bridge at Concord. Tours are self-guided and military demonstration programs in costume are scheduled throughout the summer.

Early on June 17, 1775, the quiet morning air around Charlestown Heights, just across the Charles River from Boston, was shattered by the roar of broadsides from H.M.S. *Lively*. The British were firing on the American redoubts built on Breed's pasture, the lower portion of Bunker Hill. The Revolutionary War had begun in earnest. Misnamed the Battle of Bunker Hill, this first full-scale action of the Revolution ended in defeat for the Americans, but it undoubtedly convinced the British that they were in for a long and difficult struggle. The **Bunker Hill Monument** (NHL), erected in 1825, marks the approximate center of the American redoubt. A small museum at the base has several interesting relics of the battle and honors Gen. Joseph Warren and Peter Salem, the black soldier who mortally wounded British Major Pitcairn. A 4-acre State park surrounds the monument located off of High St. and Monument Ave. in Charlestown [4].

After the Battle of Bunker Hill, the Americans settled down for a long siege of Boston. Washington was appointed commander in chief of the Continental Army in June 1775, and for the next 9 months he occupied the confiscated house of a Tory sympathizer in Cambridge [5]. Now known as the **Vassal-Craigie-Longfellow House,** it became the home of Henry Wadsworth Longfellow from 1837 to 1882. **Longfellow National Historic Site,** 105 Brattle St., is managed by the National Park Service. The house furnishings and site interpretation reflect the period of the poet's residence. (Assistance will be needed for wheelchairs.)

The seizure and fortification in March 1776 of Dorchester Heights in what is now Thomas Park, South Boston [1], was the first real stroke of military success enjoyed by the Continental Army. Not only were the British forced to evacuate Boston by this unexpected move, but the success served to inspire confidence in the leadership and capabilities of the American Army after the long siege of that city. **Dorchester Heights National Historic Site** is administered by the Boston Department of Parks.

**Adams National Historic Site,** in Quincy [6], is the home of four generations of the Adams family, the most prominent of whom was John Adams, a leading figure in the Revolution. John and his son John Quincy each served later as President of the United States. The house furnishings and site interpretation cover the Adams family through 1927 and Brooks Adams, the last to occupy the house.

Salem [7], with its sheltered harbor, was a maritime town from its beginning in the early colonial period. Shipping activity grew through the years and reached a peak in the early 1800's with the expansion of American trade that was made possible as a result of the Revolutionary War. During the Revolution, Salem, the only port of any significance not to fall into British hands, contributed to the war by supplying privateers. More than 200 Salem vessels were commissioned by the Continental Congress. They harassed the British merchant fleet in the English Channel and captured supply ships bound for Boston.

**Salem Maritime National Historic Site** is one of two National Park Service areas that emphasize the commercial and industrial aspects of the Revolution. The park includes Derby Wharf, which was built in 1762, and served as a base for outfitting privateers, and the site of prize auctions of captured British vessels and cargoes. The Derby House was the home of Elias Hasket Derby, one of the most active shipowners of the Revolutionary War period and the early years of the republic. Other structures at the park date from the era after the Revolution when Salem ships made pioneering voyages to ports in the Far East. These include the Custom House where Nathaniel Hawthorne worked as Surveyor of the Port, Bonded Warehouse with the original cargo handling equipment still in operation, Scale House, West India Goods Shop, and the Central Wharf. The park is located along the Derby Street waterfront in Salem. Periodical guided tours are given by the park staff. (Assistance will be needed for wheelchairs.)

Other Massachusetts sites associated with the Revolution are **Jason Russell House,** Arlington [8], a refuge for minutemen during the retreat of the British after the Lexington-Concord fight; **Munroe Tavern,** Lexington [2], headquarters for the British relief party during the Lexington-Concord fight; **Copps Hill,** Boston [1], famous burial ground and the place from where artillery fire was directed on Charlestown during the Battle of Bunker Hill; **General John Glover House** (private, NHL), Marblehead [9], home of the officer who directed Washington's retreat across the East River (Battle for Manhattan), August 1776, and also the crossing of the Delaware River, December 1776; **General Benjamin Lincoln House** (private, NHL), Hingham [10]; **General Rufus Putnam House** (private, NHL), Rutland [11]; and **Elmwood (Oliver-Gerry-Lowell House,** private, NHL), Cambridge [5], home of Elbridge Gerry, a Massachusetts signer of the Declaration of Independence.

Massachusetts travel, historic sites, National Park Service, and Bicentennial information can be obtained by writing to:

Massachusetts Department of Commerce and Development, Division of Tourism, Boston, MA 02105.

Adams National Historic Site, P.O. Box 531, Quincy, MA 02169

Longfellow National Historic Site, c/o Boston Group, NPS, P.O. Box 160, Concord, MA 01742.

Minute Man National Historical Park, P.O. Box 160, Concord, MA 01742.

Salem Maritime National Historical Site, P.O. Box 847, Salem, MA 01970.

The Commonwealth of Massachusetts Bicentennial Commission, 10 Tremont St., Boston, MA 02108

No military action took place in New Hampshire during the Revolution, but the colony supplied its share of officers and men, mostly in the northern campaigns: 4,000 militia, 12,497 army. Generals John Stark and John Sullivan lived in New Hampshire. Stark won his greatest fame at the Battle of Bennington. Sullivan was a member of the Second Continenal Congress and served with distinction under Washington.

## New Hampshire

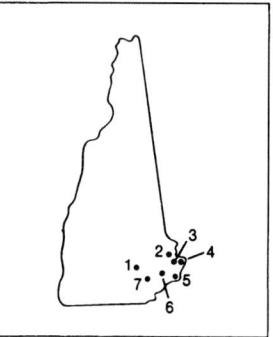

2nd New Hampshire Regiment flag, captured by British, July 1777; New Hampshire Historical Society, Concord

Gen. John Sullivan, from a sketch by Benson J Lossing.

Gen. John Stark, by U D. Tenney; General Stark House, Manchester

Moffat-Ladd House, Portsmouth.

Some of the New Hampshire sites associated with the Revolution are the **General John Stark House,** Manchester [1], home of the general after the war; **General John Sullivan House** (private, NHL), Durham [2], Sullivan's home for more than 10 years prior to the Revolution; **John Paul Jones House** (NHL), Portsmouth [3], where Jones lived during the outfitting of the *Ranger* and the *America,* 1782; **Fort Constitution,** New Castle [4], originally Fort William and Mary, renamed after the December 1774 raid by John Sullivan, one of the first armed acts of the Revolution; **Governor Meshech Weare House** (private), Hampton Falls [5], home of New Hampshire's wartime governor; and three houses associated with New Hampshire's signers of the Declaration of Independence: **Josiah Bartlett House** (private, NHL), Kingston [6], **Matthew Thornton House** (private, NHL), Derry [7], and **Moffatt-Ladd House** (NHL), Portsmouth [3], home of William Whipple.

New Hampshire travel, historic sites, and Bicentennial information can be obtained by writing to:

New Hampshire Office of Vacation Travel, Box 856, Concord, NH 03301.

New Hampshire American Revolution Bicentennial Commission, P.O. Box 856, Concord, NH 03257.

**Caught between New York and Philadelphia, New Jersey was crossed many times by elements of both the British and American armies. Often called the "cockpit of the Revolution," this small colony was divided in its loyalties and was the scene of three crucial Revolutionary War battles. New Jersey troops numbered 7,000 militia and 10,726 Continental Army.**

## New Jersey

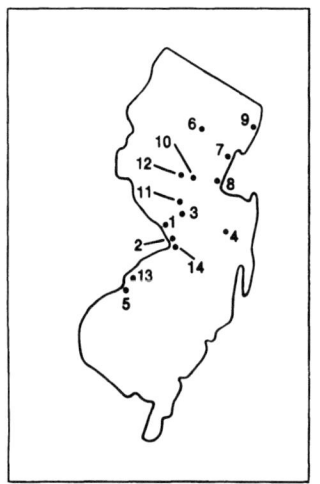

McKonkey Ferry House, Washington Crossing State Park.

Reenactment of a winter encampment at Morristown National Historical Park.

Kitchen of the Ford Mansion, Washington's Headquarters, Morristown National Historical Park.

Rockingham, Rocky Hill, Washington's Headquarters, 1783.

"Pasteboard money of the rebels;" a facsimile of Continental bills, from a sketch by Benson J. Lossing.

Washington at Monmouth,
by Emmanuel Leutze;
Monmouth County Historical
Association, Freehold.

Reconstructed log hut,
Morristown National
Historical Park

Ford Mansion, Washington's Headquarters, Morristown National Historical Park.

The Old Barracks, Trenton.

Morven, Princeton, home of Richard Stockton, New Jersey signer of the Declaration of Independence; now the governor's residence.

General Lafayette, by Charles Willson Peale.

As every schoolchild knows, George Washington crossed the Delaware on Christmas night 1776. Despite its almost legendary place in American history, largely because of the famous Emanuel Leutze painting, the crossing was actually a carefully planned maneuver designed to rescue what was rapidly becoming a lost cause. Washington and his troops landed at what is now **Washington Crossing State Park** (NHL) on the New Jersey side of the river (N.J. 546 south of Titusville [1]) and from there launched their brilliant raid on Trenton [2], a crucial episode in the Revolution. A monument to the **Battle of Trenton** stands at Broad and Warren Streets in that city. The city itself has overgrown the original battlefield. Only one building associated with the Trenton attack stands today: **The Old Barracks** (NHL), South Willow St. opposite West Front St., which was occupied by Hessian soldiers at the time of Washington's attack. (See *Pennsylvania* for the crossing point on the opposite side of the river.) After defeating the Hessians at Trenton, Washington returned to Pennsylvania only to strike again in New Jersey in a less famous Delaware crossing on the night of December 30. Facing Cornwallis, and with his back to the river, Washington daringly maneuvered around and to the rear of the British. During the night and early on the morning of January 3, he struck two British regiments that were leaving Princeton to join Cornwallis. On the verge of defeat, Washington rallied his men and drove the enemy back toward New Brunswick. One detachment of British troops sought refuge in Princeton University's **Nassau Hall** (NHL), where they were easily captured. At various times during the Revolution the hall served as a barracks and hospital for both British and American troops. The scene of the heaviest fighting during the 15-minute **Battle of Princeton** is preserved in a 40-acre State park, **Princeton Battlefield** (NHL), on N.J. 583, south edge of Princeton [3]. The **Clark House** at the edge of the field was the scene of American Gen. Hugh Mercer's death, and a memorial arch on the west edge of the battlefield marks the burial site of unknown Americans.

The **Battle of Monmouth** was the last major battle fought in the North, and it was the debut of an American army that was able to meet the British on even terms. The Continental Army had survived the hardships of Valley Forge during the winter of 1777–78 and had been trained by the Prussian drillmaster, Baron Frederick von Steuben. When British Gen. Sir Henry Clinton abandoned Philadelphia and headed for the New Jersey coast with 10,000 men, Washington and 14,000 men followed. They met on the fields around Monmouth Courthouse, N.J. 522 northwest of Freehold [4], on June 28, 1778, in the longest sustained action of the war and on the hottest day of the year. Washington failed in his attempt to prevent Clinton's escape, but he had demonstrated his own superb qualities of leadership and the new prowess of the army created at Valley Forge. The **Monmouth Battlefield** (NHL), one of the best preserved Revolutionary War battlefields, is now a New Jersey State park.

Forts Mercer (N.J.) and Mifflin (Pa.), erected to guard the Delaware River approach to Philadelphia, played a vital role in the Philadelphia campaign of 1777. Their existence caused the British commander in chief, Sir William Howe, to approach Philadelphia by the longer Chesapeake Bay route rather than the direct river approach. It then became difficult for him to return to the Hudson Valley in time to support the British army moving south from Canada. The **Battle of Red Bank** on October 22, 1777, caused Howe serious supply difficulties by blocking his direct water route to the sea even after he had captured Philadelphia. Howe had to divert considerable forces over a long period of time to take the two American posts. Extensive remains of Fort Mercer's dry ditch and earth ramparts, now grass-covered, are located in a 20-acre Gloucester County park known as **Red Bank Battlefield** (NHL), 1 mile from the town of National Park, N.J. [5].

The small community of Morristown, N.J. [6], was the scene of nearly continuous military activity from 1776 to 1782. The Continental Army spent the winters of 1776–77 and 1779–80 encamped at Morristown. From this position behind the Watchung Mountains Washington kept watch on the British Army in New York City, protected his supply and communication lines, and guarded the main roads connecting New England and Pennsylvania. From here he could move swiftly to any point threatened by the enemy.

**Morristown National Historical Park** features the unspoiled natural setting on the edge of Morristown where the Continental Army passed the winter of 1779–80. The **Ford Mansion,** Washington's headquarters, and the **Wick House** have been restored and refurnished. Log huts representing the soldiers' quarters have been reconstructed in the **Jockey Hollow** encampment area. The park museum contains many exhibits illustrating the Morristown story. The Ford Mansion is located at 230 Morris St., Morristown; Jockey Hollow, 4 miles south of Morristown. Assistance will be needed for wheelchairs at the Ford Mansion. Tours are self-guided, and throughout the spring, summer, and fall, demonstrations of military life and domestic crafts are presented in costume. Hiking is permitted in some areas.

Other New Jersey sites associated with the Revolution are **Boxwood Hall** (NHL), Elizabeth [7], home of Elias Boudinot, commissary for American prisoners held by the British and President of the Continental Congress, 1782–83; **The Proprietory House** (not open to the public), Perth Amboy [8] home of last royal governor of New Jersey, William Franklin; **Liberty Hall** (private, NHL), Elizabeth [7], home of William Livingston, political leader and New Jersey's wartime governor; **Fort Lee,** Fort Lee [9], site of the fort lost to the British November 1776; **Middlebrook Encampment,** Bound Brook [10], a base and encampment for the Continental Army in May–June 1777 and from November 1778 to June 1779; **The Hermitage** (private), Trenton [2], home of Gen. Philemon Dickinson; **Rockingham (Berrien House),** Rocky Hill [11], used as Washington's headquarters in 1783 and where he wrote his farewell speech to the army; the **Wallace House,** Somerville [12], Washington's headquarters during the Middlebrook encampment; **Indian King Tavern,** Haddonfield [13], meeting place for the New Jersey legislature, spring and fall of 1777; **Maybury Hill** (private, NHL), Princeton [3], birthplace and boyhood home of Joseph Hewes, a North Carolina signer of the Declaration of Independence; and houses associated with three of New Jersey's five signers of the Declaration of Independence: **President's House** (NHL), Princeton [3], home of John Witherspoon; **Hopkinson House** (NHL), Bordentown [14], home of Francis Hopkinson; **Morven** (NHL), Princeton [3], home of Richard Stockton, used as a headquarters by Cornwallis, and now the Governor's mansion.

New Jersey travel, historic sites, National Park Service, and Bicentennial information can be obtained by writing to:

Department of Labor and Industry, State Promotion Office, Box 400, Trenton, NJ 08625.

Morristown National Historical Park, P O Box 1136R, Morristown, NJ 07960.

New Jersey American Revolution Bicentennial Celebration Commission, Treasury Department, Willow and State Sts., Trenton, NJ 08625.

**The colony of New York, from Manhattan to Lake Champlain and from Fort Niagara on Lake Ontario to the Pennsylvania border, was involved in nearly every major northern campaign. Albany, the capital, was the target of two major British offensives from Canada; the Hudson River Valley, considered the key to control of the North, was occupied by both armies and the subject of land battles, naval attacks, and betrayal; and the central and western wildernesses saw the war's largest single campaign**

## New York

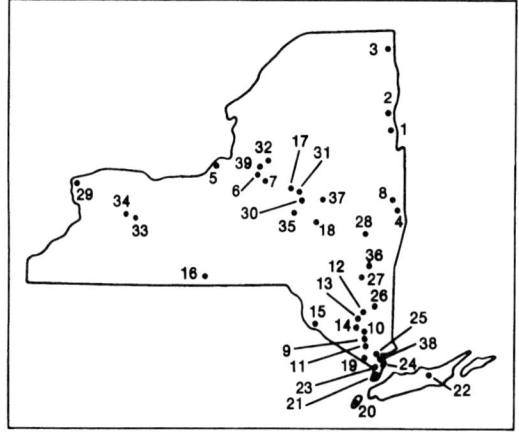

South Barracks, Fort Ticonderoga.

Living history program, Saratoga National Historical Park.

against Indians. New York began the Revolutionary War historic site preservation movement in 1850 with the preservation of Washington's headquarters at Newburgh. Today no less than 40 sites are recognized as important landmarks, and nearly 100 others are preserved in one form or another. New York gave 17,781 men to the Continental Army, with 10,000 militia.

Ruins of Crown Point.

Fort Ticonderoga.

The Capture of Major André, copied from Durand's 16-inch porcelain plate; L. V. Case Collection in the Historical Society of the Tarrytowns.

Reconstructed Temple, New Windsor Cantonment, New Windsor.

Hasbrouck House, or Washington's Headquarters, Newburgh, as seen by Benson J. Lossing in 1848, just prior to its dedication as a historic site.

Raising the Stars and Stripes over Fort Stanwix, August 3, 1777, by Edward Buyck, Fort Stanwix Museum

Indian Chief Joseph Brant, by Charles Willson Peale.

Thaddeus Kosciuszko, Polish officer at Saratoga; U.S. Capitol, Washington, D.C.

A reproduction of the gold medal presented to Gen. Horatio Gates by the Continental Congress following the American victory at Saratoga.

Gen. John Burgoyne, by Sir Joshua Reynolds.

Schuyler House, Schuylerville.

The smoke had hardly cleared from the Lexington Green in Massachusetts when on May 10, 1775, Ethan Allen and the Green Mountain Boys rowed across Lake Champlain and, without firing a shot, captured **Fort Ticonderoga** (NHL). For the British there was little doubt that the American uprising was a serious rebellion The war had spread from the confines of Massachusetts; now New York was involved. Fort Ticonderoga changed hands several times during the war, but not before its cannon were hauled off across the snow-covered mountains to be used in the American siege of Boston. The fort, one of the best preserved and restored colonial military reservations, is located on N.Y. 73 just east of the village of Ticonderoga [1], 20 miles east of Exit 28, Int. 87 and is managed by a private corporation. It has a vast amount of Revolutionary War relics and artifacts. **Crown Point Reservation** (NHL), 9 miles north of the village of Crown Point at the Lake Champlain Bridge [2], a New York State historic site dating to 1731, served as an outpost for Ticonderoga. Just to the north of Fort Ticonderoga, off N.Y. 22, is **Mount Hope** [1], which overlooks the portage between Lakes Champlain and George. The blockhouse there, now reconstructed, was a strategic outpost for Fort Ticonderoga and changed hands as often as the fort. Directly across the lake, and once linked to Fort Ticonderoga by a "boat bridge," stands **Mount Independence** [1], the least disturbed of any Revolutionary War site in the country. Military roads, gun emplacements, building foundations, and graves of American soldiers are virtually untouched.

   North of Ticonderoga, near Plattsburgh [3], is **Valcour Bay** (NHL), a small body of water separating the western New York shore of Lake Champlain and Valcour Island. Here on October 11 1776, Benedict Arnold and a tiny American fleet of gunboats challenged Sir Guy Carleton's British fleet of warships that had set out from Canada for Albany to join up with a land force from New York in an attempt to divide the colonies. Although the area remains much as it was at the time, only the island stands as a memorial to one of the bloodiest engagements with perhaps the most far-reaching effects of the war. Arnold lost the **Battle of Valcour Bay,** but Carleton turned back, thus stalling invasion plans and giving the Americans another year of preparation before the British again tried the same strategy. (See the gondola *Philadelphia,* Smithsonian Institution, District of Columbia).

   In late July 1777, Gen. John Burgoyne launched his campaign to accomplish what Carleton had failed to do. He sailed down

Lake Champlain and marched down the east side of the Hudson toward Albany, where he hoped to meet Sir William Howe with his troops from New York. Four major engagements took place before Burgoyne got as far as Saratoga and the battle in which he was ultimately defeated: **Hubbardton** in Vermont, and **Bennington, Fort Stanwix** and **Oriskany** in New York. (See **Vermont** for the **Battle of Hubbardton.**) In mid-August Burgoyne sent a detachment of Hessian troops toward Bennington, Vt., to capture much needed supplies. A small American force under Gen. John Stark met the enemy at a field just 2 miles inside the New York border on August 16 and soundly defeated them in two engagements. Called the **Battle of Bennington** (NHL), the field along N.Y. 67, about 1 mile east of Waloomsac [4], has been preserved and marked by the State of New York.

While Burgoyne marched south along the Hudson, Col. Barry St. Leger was to strike out from **Fort Ontario,** Oswego [5], march down the Mohawk Valley, and join the others at Albany. On August 2, St. Leger laid siege to the newly rebuilt and occupied Fort Stanwix.

**Fort Stanwix National Monument,** located in downtown Rome, N.Y. [6], marks the site of a British fort built in 1758 on a strategic location overlooking the Mohawk River and Wood Creek Portage. Used during the French and Indian War, it was inactive for some years, but with the coming of the Revolution, American leaders recognized its strategic importance and quickly moved to make repairs. By August 1, 1777, it was again defensible and successfully held off St. Leger's siege.

Gen. Nicholas Herkimer led the Tryon County Militia to the aid of the men at Stanwix, but on August 6, at Oriskany, about 6 miles from the fort, Herkimer's force was ambushed by St. Leger's men and driven back with heavy losses. The British maintained the siege of Fort Stanwix, but they were unable to mount an assault.

Finally, on August 23, faced with the wholesale desertion of his Indian allies and the approach of an American relief column under Benedict Arnold, St. Leger abandoned operations and retired to Canada. The failure to take Fort Stanwix deterred Burgoyne's campaign and contributed greatly to his defeat at Saratoga in October. Fort Stanwix is presently being excavated by the National Park Service. The Fort Stanwix Museum, under private sponsorship, nearby on Spring St. in Rome, offers interpretation of the fort and its history. The **Oriskany Battlefield**

(NHL) [7], along N.Y. 69 between Oriskany and Rome, is today owned and preserved by the State of New York.

On the heights just south of Saratoga in the fall of 1777 an interesting mixture of troops daring to call themselves an American army defeated the flower of England's armed might under Burgoyne in what has been termed one of the most significant military engagements in history. Gen. Horatio Gates' decisive victory and the resulting surrender of Burgoyne's army realized the immediate American objectives of preventing British control of the strategic Hudson River Valley and the military isolation of the New England colonies. Yet the victory had more far-reaching effects. The surrender of Burgoyne and his army not only restored the sagging confidence of the Americans in their own military abilities when most needed, but it also brought recognition and assistance from France—assistance that made possible the final victory at Yorktown 4 years later.

Some of the great men of the Continental Army fought here: Horatio Gates, who directed the American forces; Daniel Morgan, whose rifle corps opened the fight at the Freeman Farm; Benedict Arnold, whose assault on the Breymann Redoubt was an important factor in the battle; and Thaddeus Kosciuszko, the Polish military engineer, who selected and fortified the American lines.

**Saratoga National Historical Park** preserves more than 2,000 acres of the rolling countryside along the Hudson where the two armies battled. Paved roads provide a self-guided tour route to the sites of action, and to the opposing redoubts, fortifications, and military headquarters, all of which are identified and interpreted.

The main entrance to Saratoga National Historical Park is 30 miles north of Albany on U.S. 4 and N.Y. 32 [8]. Handicapped persons will have difficulties moving from the parking lot to the visitor center and in reaching the Arnold Monument at Stop 7. Programs of military and domestic craft demonstrations are presented throughout the summer.

A 25-acre detached section of the park at nearby Schuylerville [8] includes the restored and refurnished **Schuyler House** (NHL), summer residence of Gen. Philip Schuyler, who relinquished command of the American force to General Gates almost on the eve of the Battle of Saratoga. The ceremony of surrender by the British took place at the Field of Grounded Arms, not a part of the park, at Schuylerville.

During Burgoyne's fight with Gates' forces at Saratoga, British Gen. Sir Henry Clinton led an expedition into the Hudson

Highlands and attacked Forts Clinton and Montgomery, two strong points controlling the Hudson River. His object was to create such a diversion that Gates would be forced to send troops south from Saratoga and thus take some of the pressure off Burgoyne. Gates did dispatch some men, but not enough to harm

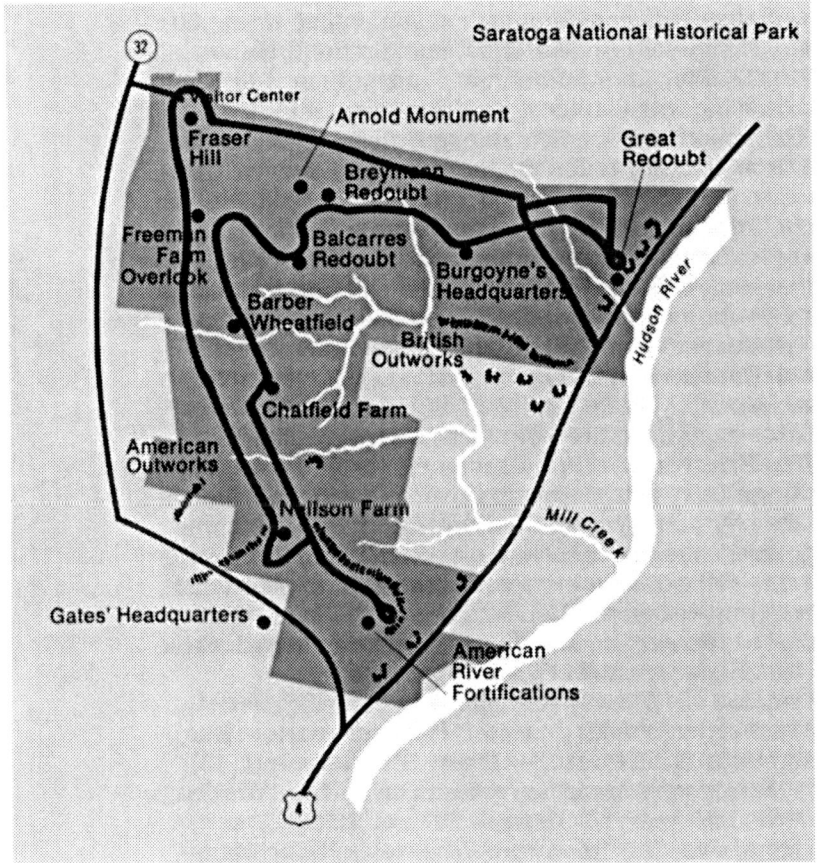

his position at Saratoga. On October 6, 1777, Clinton's forces took these forts and on October 7 they broke the defensive boom across the river. This was the extent of Clinton's activities. The Bear Mountain Historical Museum (Bear Mountain State Park), off U.S. 9W near Bear Mountain Bridge [9], is on the site of **Fort Clinton,** and it contains exhibits on the history of both forts as well as artifacts associated with those who fought there. The ruins of

**Fort Montgomery** (NHL) are the subject of intensive archeological studies.

West Point [10] was the focal point of one of the best known stories of the Revolution, the treason of Benedict Arnold. Arnold was given command of the West Point fortifications on August 3, 1780. For more than a year, however, he had been secretly negotiating with the British, and once in command he arranged with Sir Henry Clinton to turn over West Point to the British in return for £20,000. Maj. John André, the British officer with whom he had been dealing, was captured, and Arnold's plot was revealed. On September 25, Arnold fled to a British warship in the Hudson and from that day fought on the side of the enemy. The British, however, did not fully trust him, and when Arnold and his wife moved to England in 1781, they were scorned and neglected. Arnold died a broken, penniless, bitter man. The West Point Museum at the United States Military Academy (NHL) has a large collection of Revolutionary war relics. The remains of fortifications at **Fort Putnam** and on **Constitution Island** can be seen.

**Stony Point Battlefield Reservation** (NHL) is just a few miles south of Bear Mountain State Park, just off U.S. 9W [11]. One of the most daring exploits of the Revolution took place there in July 1779. The British sat securely behind the fortifications and controlled Kings Ferry on the Hudson River, a key to the Hudson Highlands. Gen. Anthony Wayne, in a surprise attack using only bayonets (to avoid a telltale accidental shot), took the Point after midnight on the 16th with hand-to-hand combat. It was here that Wayne earned the nickname "Mad Anthony," and it was this daring attack that earned him a gold medal and the thanks of the Congress. The original earthworks are still visible.

The first months of 1783 were among the most trying periods of George Washington's military career. His headquarters was located at the Hasbrouck House, 84 Liberty St., Newburgh [12], and his army was encamped a few miles away at New Windsor on Temple Hill Road between N.Y. Routes 207 and 32 [13]. The Hasbrouck House was the first place in the Nation to be recognized formally by a State government as a historic site (1850), and today, known as **Washington's Headquarters** (NHL), it is a memorial to Washington and the Revolution. A fine museum, operated by the State, houses a large collection of Revolutionary War artifacts. It was during the **New Windsor Cantonment,** or encampment, that Washington's officers circulated their "Newburgh Letters" threatening mutiny. In one of the most moving moments of the closing hours of the Revolution, Washington assembled his men in the Temple or meeting house at the Cantonment and in a personal appeal asked the men to be patient. His words were heeded. One of the Cantonment's original 700 wooden huts has survived. Other buildings on the grounds are reconstructions. Administered by the State, the Cantonment offers military demonstrations daily from April to November. Nearby, at Vails Gate [14], on Forge Hill Road, is the **Knox Headquarters** (NHL), used at various times by Washington's artillery commander, Gen. Henry Knox, between June 1779 and September 1782. The house was also used by Generals Greene, Steuben, and Gates.

Not all Revolutionary War military action was between the American forces and the British. In many areas Tories allied themselves with various Indian tribes and played havoc with anyone who showed any patriot leanings. This was particularly prevalent in New York. **Minisink Battlefield,** along the New York-Pennsylvania border just north of Minisink Ford, N.Y. and Lackawaxen, Pa. [15], was the scene of a Tory-patriot engagement on July 22, 1779. A force of Tories and Indians under the Mohawk Chief Joseph Brant surprised the sleeping village of Minisink on the night of July 19, withdrawing after burning and looting the village. About 150 local militiamen set out after them and were ambushed near a ford on the Delaware River. At least 45 Americans were killed before both forces retired from the field.

In some respects the action at **Newtown Battlefield** (NHL), about 5 miles east of Elmira on N.Y. 17 [16], was similar. Here on August 29, 1779, an expeditionary force under Generals John Sullivan and James Clinton defeated a force of Tories and Indians under the command of Col. John Butler and the Indian chief Joseph Brant. The **Battle of Newton** was the last major Tory effort to halt the Sullivan-Clinton Expedition, which continued on to destroy Indian villages on New York's western frontier. Both battlefields have been set aside as historic monuments and are open to the public.

New York is dotted with historic houses and fortifications associated with the Revolution, ranging from the Hudson Valley to the western frontier, and including Manhattan and Long Island. Gen. Nicholas Herkimer's fame came when his troops confronted Col. Barry St. Leger's British regulars, Tories, and Indians at the Battle of Oriskany. Herkimer's home and burial site are located on N.Y. 5S about 2 miles east of Little Falls [17].

**Old Stone Fort,** just off N.Y. 30 at Schoharie [18], was, in 1778, a church converted to a fort, enclosed by a log stockade and supported by two log blockhouses. Known as the Lower Fort, it served as a place of refuge for residents of the Schoharie Valley and as a fortification against Tory and Indian raids. The largest attack on the fort came on October 17, 1780, when Sir John Johnson led a force of 800 Tories and Indians against it. Today the church is a museum and still bears the scars of the attack.

During the Revolution the **De Wint House (George Washington Masonic Shrine),** Livingston Ave. and Oak Tree Rd., Tappan [19], served several times as General Washington's headquarters. He was here at the time of the trial and execution of Maj. John André, Benedict Arnold's co-conspirator in the plot against West Point. The De Wint House (NHL) is furnished much as it was at the time of the war. Nearby is the **76 House** in which André was imprisoned and the **Tappan Reformed (Dutch) Church** where his court-martial trial was held.

On September 11, 1776, John Adams, Benjamin Franklin, and Edward Rutledge, representing the Continental Congress, met with British Adm. Lord Richard Howe at the Billopp House, Staten Island, to discuss possible peace negotiations. Lord Howe demanded the repudiation of the Declaration of Independence and the disbanding of the Continental Army. The Americans rejected the proposals and returned to Philadelphia. Now called the **Conference House** (NHL), located at 7455 Hylan Blvd., Tottenville [20], it has been restored as a museum and is furnished in the style of the Revolutionary War period.

**The Battle for Manhattan**

Throughout the Revolutionary War the Hudson River and its valley held a special attraction for the British. Not only was it a direct route to and from Canada and a base for military operations, but it served as a means of dividing the colonies, a prime objective of British military strategy. And at the mouth of the Hudson lay New York City [21], a large island containing farms for provisions and ample lands for troop encampments. Of great importance to the British navy, it was also surrounded by navigable waters. By 1776, the British had already suffered defeat at Boston and were forced to evacuate the city. Gen. Sir William Howe took his troops first to Halifax, Nova Scotia, and then to New York. By July Howe had 32,000 professional soldiers on Staten Island including, for the first time, German mercenaries, and 200 ships of various sizes and types in the lower harbor.

More than anyone else, Washington knew the value of the Hudson. He also knew the condition of his own army—19,000 raw troops that were untrained, undisciplined, and, at best, only willing to serve out their short-term enlistments. These disadvantages against the fresh, well-trained British army clearly forewarned what was to come in battle. At all costs, however, Washington had to keep the Hudson River free of British warships.

On August 22, Howe began ferrying his troops across the Narrows to Long Island. By the 25th all had landed at what is now Dyker Beach Park. The landing was unopposed. The Americans were manning crude redoubts on Brooklyn Heights, with a battery at what is now Prospect Park. Just behind this vulnerable position was the East River.

The British attack came shortly before midnight on the 26th. Two columns engaged the Americans at their front batteries while a third moved around to the right to encircle Washington's troops. Outnumbered, the Americans retreated to the redoubts on Brooklyn Heights before the trap could be completed. Faced with having to make a frontal assault, Howe waited. A storm came up that prevented British ships from using the East River, giving Washington his chance to escape. Throughout the night of the 29th small boats carried 9,500 of Washington's men across the river to Manhattan. The Americans were defeated and Washington himself narrowly missed being captured. The British had won the first phase of the battle for Manhattan.

By the time Howe landed in Manhattan 2 weeks later, Washington had decided to give up the island. His decision came a little too late, however, and on Sunday morning, September 15, when Howe stormed ashore at Kip's Bay, at the foot of what is now 34th Street, Washington still had some troops in the vicinity. He had fully expected Howe to invade in the Harlem area, and, as a matter of fact, his own headquarters were at the **Morris-Jumel Mansion** (NHL), still standing on 161st Street overlooking the Polo Grounds. The Connecticut troops on the Kip farm were green, some even without uniforms. The awesome sight of the British landing was too much for them and they broke and ran, heading north along what is now Lexington Avenue.

Washington, hearing sounds of the battle, left Harlem Heights with reinforcements to try to rally his retreating men in a cornfield near present Grand Central Station, but the demoralized Connecticut troops raced around him despite his shouts and warnings. To preserve some order, the troops were directed on to Harlem

Heights and safety. Although there was some rear-guard skirmishing, most of the men reached Harlem by nightfall, exhausted and hungry, but with surprisingly few casualties. Almost all of the farms along the way, however, had experienced some ravaging. The British followed on a route that now goes near the United Nations and diagonally across Central Park to 120th Street

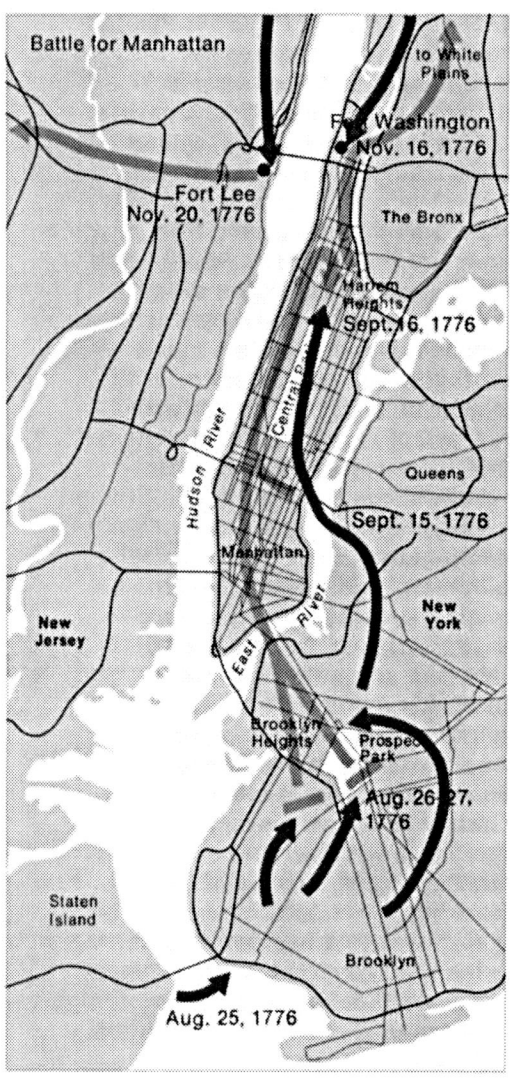

Early the next morning scouts advanced silently out from Harlem Heights onto an area on Morningside Heights now occupied by Columbia University's Barnard College, and the Cathedral of St. John the Divine. Here the Americans enticed the British to show themselves and slowly led them back to what is now Riverside Drive, Broadway and 120th Street, near Grant's Tomb. For several hours throughout the morning the situation was dangerously close to breaking into open battle, something Washington did not want and was not prepared for. About noon, however, the British held back. For the next several months the two lines stared at each other while Howe prepared for a flanking movement by way of the East River and Pell's Point. Some attempts were made against Washington's flanks but the bulk of the American army moved north to White Plains. Only token forces were left behind to guard Fort Washington, near the present George Washington Bridge, and Fort Lee, almost directly across the Hudson on the palisades of New Jersey.

Washington and Howe faced each other again on October 28 at White Plains. The Americans were again defeated. Fort Washington was captured on November 16 and Fort Lee a short time later. Howe gave up trying to get around and in back of Washington, whose Continentals retreated across the Hudson and into New Jersey. The Battle of Manhattan was over. The British had taken the island and for the moment were satisfied. Washington's army was rapidly dwindling through desertions. The future looked bleak. But Christmas Day and the crossing of the Delaware to a magnificent victory at Trenton were yet to come.

Although they were not involved in military action, there are three historic sites in Manhattan closely related to persons and events surrounding the Revolutionary period.

Hamilton Grange, built in 1801, was the only home Alexander Hamilton ever owned. Hamilton, best known for his position as first Secretary of the Treasury and his strong Federalist philosophy, served as aide-de-camp to Washington and as an artillery officer during the Revolution. The house, located at 287 Convent Ave., is now **Hamilton Grange National Memorial** and is administered by the National Park Service. Assistance will be needed for wheelchair visitors.

On the site of the present Federal Hall, 26 Wall St., stood the old City Hall that served as a meeting place for the Stamp Act Congress in 1765 and the Continental Congress between 1785 and 1788. A year later it became the first Capitol of the United

States under the Constitution. A number of pre-Revolutionary War events concerning human liberties and freedom of speech took place here, including the trial and acquittal of John Peter Zenger in 1735 in his fight for freedom of the press. On its balcony George Washington was inaugurated in 1789 as the first President of the United States. The present structure was built in 1842 as a customhouse. **Federal Hall National Memorial** is administered by the National Park Service. Guided tours are given periodically. Wheelchair visitors must use the ramp at the rear entrance on Pine Street.

**Fraunces Tavern,** 54 Pearl St., was built in 1719 and acquired some years before the Revolution by Samuel Fraunces, whose tavern became a favorite meeting place. On December 7, 1783, it was the scene of Washington's farewell to the officers of the Continental Army. The building has gone through a number of structural changes. In 1907 it was restored to its original appearance by the Sons of the Revolution and today serves as their headquarters.

Other New York sites associated with the Revolution are **Raynham Hall,** Oyster Bay, Long Island [22], military headquarters for British Lt. Col. John Granes Simcoe during the winter of 1778 and the place where Benedict Arnold met British spy John André; **Philipse Manor Hall** (NHL), Yonkers [23], occupied by both sides and sometime headquarters for British Gen. Sir Henry Clinton, 1778–81; **Thomas Paine Cottage** (NHL), New Rochelle [24], home of the master pamphleteer and Revolutionary War propagandist, 1802–6; **Washington's Headquarters,** North White Plains [25], used as the general's headquarters three times during the war, 1776, 1778 and 1781; **Van Wyck Homestead Museum,** Fishkill [26], all that remains of the massive American supply depot and military encampment at Fishkill; **Senate House,** Kingston [27], site of the meeting of the first New York State Senate, February 1777; **Historic Cherry Hill,** Albany [28], home of Col. Philip Van Rensselaer, commissary of military stores in New York during the Revolution; **The Pastures** (Schuyler Mansion) (NHL), Albany [28], home of Gen. Philip Schuyler; **Old Fort Niagara,** Youngstown [29], British stronghold and base for guerrilla warfare against New York and Pennsylvania; **Saratoga Battle Monument and Field of Grounded Arms,** Schuylerville [8]; **Fort Plain Museum,** Fort Plain [30], headquarters for the American defense of the Mohawk Valley; **Fort Klock** (NHL), St. Johnsville [31], site of the **Battle of Klock's Field.** October 19. 1780: **Baron Von Steuben Memorial.**

Remsen [32], land and replica of cabin given to Steuben by the State of New York in gratitude for his services, and Steuben's grave; **Groveland Ambuscade Park,** Groveland [33], commemorating the Sullivan-Clinton expedition against the Iroquois Indians in 1779, **Boyd-Parker Memorial Park,** Cuylerville [34], the site where Lt. Thomas Boyd and Sgt. Michael Parker of Sullivan's expedition were ambushed and tortured to death by the Indians; **Cherry Valley Massacre Site,** Cherry Valley [35], site of the massacre of women and children by a British-inspired Indian raid; **Clermont** (NHL), Tivoli-on-the-Hudson [36], home of Robert R. Livingston II, political leader and first Secretary of Foreign Affairs during the Revolution; **Fort Johnson** (NHL), Fort Johnson [37], fortified home of Sir William Johnson, British Indian Commissioner, and later the home of his son John, a soldier and Loyalist leader in the Revolution; **Sagtikos Manor,** Bay Shore, Long Island [22], headquarters of British General Clinton during the Revolution; **Bush Homestead,** Port Chester [38], Gen. Israel Putnam's headquarters, 1777–78; and two houses associated with William Floyd, a New York signer of the Declaration of Independence: **Gen. William Floyd House** (private, NHL), Westernville [39], and the **William Floyd House** (private), Mastic, Long Island [22] (in Fire Island National Seashore).

New York travel, historic sites, National Park Service, and Bicentennial information can be obtained by writing to.

Travel Bureau, New York State Department of Commerce, 99 Washington Ave., Albany, NY 12210

Fort Stanwix National Monument, c/o New York District Office, NPS, 26 Wall St., New York, NY 10005

Saratoga National Historical Park, R D 1, Box 113-C, Stillwater, NY 12170.

Federal Hall National Monument, 26 Wall St., New York, NY 10005

Hamilton Grange National Memorial, c/o Manhattan Group, NPS, 26 Wall St., New York, NY 10005

New York State American Revolution Bicentennial Commission, Office of State History, State Education Department, 99 Washington Ave., Albany, NY 12210

War reached North Carolina early in the Revolutionary years, but from internal strife rather than British forces. Virtually a civil uprising, the Battle of Moores Creek set the tone for southern sympathies and pushed North Carolina's delegates to the Continental Congress to be the first to urge independence. Not until the British launched their Southern Campaign in the latter part of the war did this colony again become involved in hostilities. Savannah fell in 1778 and Charleston in 1780. Then

## North Carolina

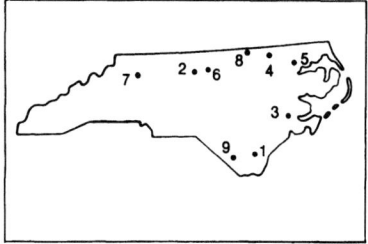

Joseph Hewes, North Carolina signer of the Declaration of Independence, a miniature by Charles Willson Peale

Nash-Hooper House, Hillsborough

Cornwallis moved north. Talented and capable officers like Nathanael Greene and Daniel Morgan sparred across the Piedmont with the British in a series of battles and skirmishes that led Cornwallis to Yorktown. "We fight, get beat, rise and fight again," wrote Greene. North Carolina Continentals numbered 7,263, with 13,000 militia on the home front.

John Penn, North Carolina signer of the Declaration of Independence.

Excavation, Brunswick Town State Historic Site, Brunswick.

Guilford Courthouse Flag, reputed to have been carried during battle; North Carolina Hall of History, Raleigh.

North Carolina militia drum; Guilford Courthouse National Military Park.

North Carolina patriots and Loyalists clashed at Moores Creek Bridge on February 27, 1776, in one of the first critical actions of the American Revolution. Here patriot militia under Col. Richard Caswell and Col. Alexander Lillington threw back a larger Loyalist force on its way to rendezvous with a British expeditionary squadron on the coast. Small as the battle was, it had a crucial importance. The victory helped prevent a full-scale invasion of the South; it caused North Carolina, on April 12, 1776, to instruct its delegation in the Continental Congress to vote for independence, the first colony to do so; and it supplied a needed stimulus for the country as a whole in the movement toward severing ties with Britain.

The size of **Moores Creek National Military Park** belies the significance of the site. The battle area administered by the National Park Service covers less than 50 acres and is nearly as remote today as it was 2 centuries ago. The battlefield is located about 20 miles northwest of Wilmington, via U.S. 421 and N.C. 210, in Pender County, near the community of Currie [1]. The park has a self-guiding trail leading to the patriot fortifications, cannon, field exhibits, monuments, and markers which tell the story of the battle.

On March 15, 1781, Gen. Nathanael Greene's forces met the British regulars under Lord Cornwallis in hand-to-hand combat at Guilford Courthouse, near present-day Greensboro. The hotly contested struggle ended in a stalemate. At the close of the day, the American forces withdrew and the British claimed a measure of success. But they had suffered so severely that Charles James Fox, the British statesman, proclaimed that "another such victory will ruin the British army." His army crippled, Cornwallis soon withdrew to Wilmington where his troops rested. He then moved into Virginia and on to Yorktown.

**Guilford Courthouse National Military Park,** on U.S. 220, 6 miles north of downtown Greensboro [2], includes the most important parts of the battlefield. A self-guiding auto tour covers the three American lines and the courthouse site. Self-guiding walking and bike trails connect the American positions. Also in the park is the grave site of John Penn and William Hooper, two of North Carolina's signers of the Declaration of Independence. Twenty-five other monuments and markers honor the participants of the battle and identify points of interest, and a visitor center interprets the action and its significance. During summer weekends military and domestic crafts demonstrations are presented.

Other North Carolina sites associated with the Revolution are **Tryon Palace,** New Bern [3], a reconstruction of the Royal Governor's palace at the outbreak of the Revolution; **Historic Halifax,** Halifax [4], marking the site of the "Halifax Resolves," the first official State action for independence, April 12, 1776, including **Loretta,** the home of Gen. William R. Davie, and the traditional **Constitution House** where the first North Carolina constitution was drafted; **Hayes** (private), Edenton [5], home of political leader Samuel Johnston; **James Iredell House** (private), Edenton [5], home of a political leader; **Hartsease, Gov. Thomas Burke-Dennis Hart House** (private), Hillsborough [6], home of wartime governor Thomas Burke; **Fort Defiance,** Lenoir [7], home of Gen. William Lenoir; **Ordinary,** Littleton [8], home of wartime governor Thomas Person; **Brunswick Town State Historic Site,** Brunswick [9]; and **Nash-Hooper House** (private, NHL), Hillsborough [6], home of William Hooper, a North Carolina signer of the Declaration of Independence.

North Carolina travel, historic sites, National Park Service, and Bicentennial information can be obtained by writing to:

Travel and Promotion Division, State Department of Natural and Economic Resources, Administration Building, Raleigh, NC 27602.

Moores Creek National Military Park, Currie NC 28435.

Guilford Courthouse National Military Park, P.O. Box 9334, Plaza Station, Greensboro, NC 27408.

North Carolina American Revolution Bicentennial Commission, Department of Art, Culture and History, 109 East Jones St., Raleigh, NC 27601.

Containing a large Loyalist population and influenced by its many Quakers, Pennsylvania was late in joining the Revolutionary movement. With the aid of such leaders as John Dickinson and Thomas Mifflin, however, the colony signed the Declaration of Independence at the State House in Philadelphia and by September 1776 had overthrown its proprietary government and adopted a new State constitution. The two Continental Congresses (1774 and 1775-81) were held in Philadelphia. During

## Pennsylvania

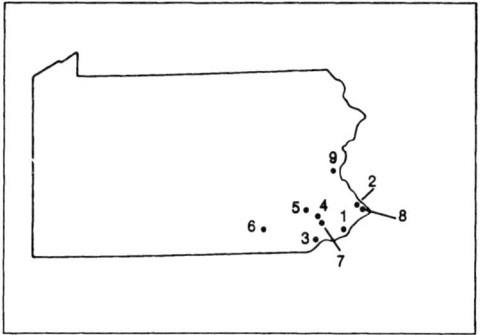

Declaration of Independence by John Trumbull; Rotunda, U S Capitol, Washington, D.C.

the British occupation of that city, Congress moved to two other locations in Pennsylvania: Lancaster and York. The Pennsylvania Line under Anthony Wayne, the navy, and the militia comprised Pennsylvania's defense force. Pennsylvania troops numbered 10,000 militia and 25,678 army. In 1777 battles were fought at Brandywine, Paoli, Fort Mifflin, and Germantown.

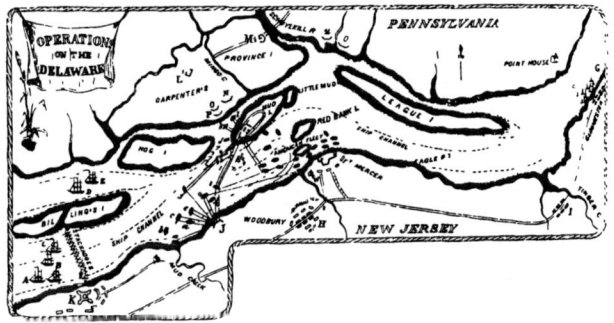

Crossing the Delaware, a bronze relief panel on the Trenton, N.J., Battle monument, by Thomas Eakins.

Assembly Room, Independence Hall.

House of Representatives Chamber, Congress Hall, Independence National Historical Park.

Operations on the Delaware River, October and November, 1777.

Cannon at Valley Forge

Washington's Headquarters, Valley Forge

Delaware River crossing site, Washington Crossing State Park.

Fort Mifflin, Philadelphia.

George Washington Reviewing his Troops at Valley Forge, by W. L Trego; Valley Forge Historical Society Museum

Independence Hall and the North Mall.

General Von Steuben, from a sketch by Benson J. Lossing.

Reconstructed soldiers' huts at Valley Forge.

Silver inkstand used in the signing of the Declaration of Independence, Independence Hall.

Warning inspired by the Stamp Act; *Pennsylvania Journal*, 1765

Benjamin Franklin's popular cartoon which appeared first in his *Pennsylvania Gazette*. 1754

**Independence Hall** is the heart of **Independence National Historical Park** in Philadelphia [1], and one of the most significant historical sites in the Nation. It was originally the statehouse for the Colony of Pennsylvania, built beginning in 1732. The Second Continental Congress met in Independence Hall in May 1775 and took the crucial steps that converted a protest movement into a resistance and independence movement. Fighting had already broken out in Massachusetts when this Congress met, and in June 1775, they chose George Washington to be general and commander in chief of the Continental Army. A year later, on July 4, 1776, the Declaration of Independence was adopted by Congress meeting here.

During the War for Independence and the ensuing period under the Articles of Confederation, except for the British occupation of this city in 1777–78, Congress met in Philadelphia, the capital of the United States. In 1783 it moved to New York City. Beginning on May 25, 1787, the Federal Constitutional Convention met here under Washington, who was president of the Convention. Benjamin Franklin, Alexander Hamilton, James Madison, and other eminent leaders made up the Convention, which labored for 4 months writing the Constitution.

Besides Independence Hall, the National Historical Park includes a number of other historic structures. Those in the Independence Hall group are owned by the City of Philadelphia and administered by the National Park Service; others are owned and occupied by certain associations. **Carpenters' Hall** (NHL) is among the most important of the latter. It was built in 1770 as a guildhall for the Carpenters' Company of Philadelphia and was the setting for the First Continental Congress in September 1774. This building is open to the public and is located in Carpenters' Court off Chestnut Street between Third and Fourth Streets.

The buildings most closely associated with the Nation's founding are on Independence Square. The former **County Court Building** is on the west, the **Old City Hall** on the east, with the **American Philosophical Society Building (Philosophical Hall)** next to it. All but Old City Hall were completed before 1790 when Philadelphia became the Federal Capital. During this period the courthouse became known as **Congress Hall** because the legislature met there and, similarly, City Hall in 1791 became the **Supreme Court Building.** Philosophical Hall is not open to the public. It is still the headquarters of the American Philosophical Society, founded in 1743 by Benjamin Franklin.

Other places associated with Independence National Historical Park include: The **First Bank of the United States,** erected in 1795–97; the **Second Bank of the United States,** 1819–24; **Philadelphia Exchange,** 1832–34; **Bishop White House,** 1786–87; **Todd House,** 1775; **New Hall,** 1790, now the Marine Corps Memorial Museum; **Pemberton House,** 1775, now the Army-Navy Museum; **Library Hall,** 1789–90; **City Tavern** site, 1775; **Franklin Court,** site of Benjamin Franklin's home from 1763 to 1790; site of the **Graff**

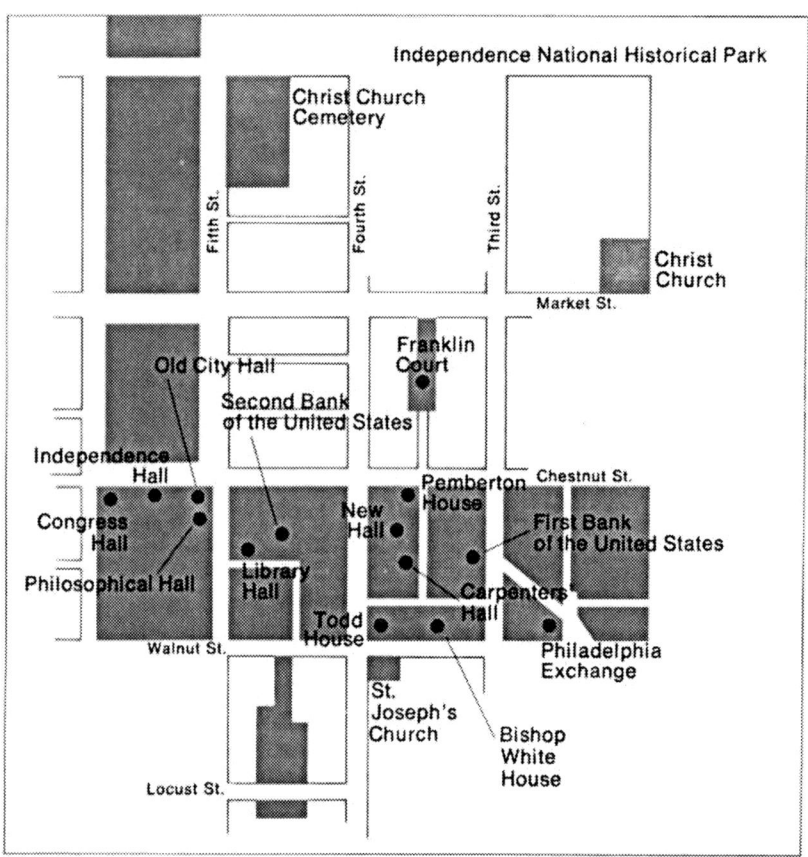

**House,** 1775, where Jefferson drafted the Declaration of Independence; **Christ Church** (NHL), 1727–54; **St. Joseph's Church** established 1733 as first Roman Catholic Church in Philadelphia (present structure, 1838); **St. Mary's Church,** established in 1763;

**St. George's Church,** 1769; **Mikveh Israel Cemetery,** 1738; **Gloria Dei (Old Swedes') Church National Historic Site** (NHL), 1700; and **Deshler-Morris House,** 5442 Germantown Ave., erected 1772–73. The famed **Liberty Bell** is displayed in Independence National Historical Park.

Independence National Historical Park is located between Walnut and Chestnut Streets and Second and Sixth Streets in Philadelphia [1]. Guided tours are given periodically through Independence Hall. Entrances to most buildings will present some difficulties for wheelchairs.

War first came to Pennsylvania with Washington's crossing of the Delaware River on Christmas night 1776. With the fruits of this initiative, Washington gave the Nation and the army a taste of victory at the lowest ebb of the patriot cause. Although the military action took place at Trenton on the New Jersey shore, Pennsylvania commemorates the embarkation point with a 478-acre State park, in which are preserved some of the buildings associated with the brief encampment there. **Washington Crossing State Park** (NHL), is located on Pa. 32 and 532, on the Delaware River at Washington Crossing, Bucks County [2]. (See **Washington Crossing State Park** in New Jersey.) A visitor center was constructed there especially to house the famed Emmanuel Leutze painting, a faithful copy of which now hangs in the auditorium. (The original painting is in the Metropolitan Museum of Art, New York City.)

American and British forces clashed in Pennsylvania at the **Battle of Brandywine** on September 11, 1777, when Sir William Howe moved his troops up the Chesapeake Bay and marched across Maryland and Delaware toward Philadelphia. This was the only major clash of the armies during this campaign. Although the Americans were defeated, Washington extricated his troops in good order. A 50-acre State park (**Brandywine Battlefield,** NHL) overlooking Chadds Ford and the main battle areas, on U.S. 1 in Delaware County [3], includes the restored quarters of the Marquis de Lafayette and a reconstruction of Washington's headquarters.

The British occupied Philadelphia on September 26, 1777, stationing about 9,000 troops in Germantown, a small village to the northwest of Philadelphia, but now within the city limits [1]. On October 4 Washington attacked in a brilliantly planned but poorly executed maneuver that centered around the house owned by Benjamin Chew on Germantown Avenue between

Johnson and Cliveden Streets. Although Washington narrowly failed to win a significant victory here, this battle and Burgoyne's surrender at Saratoga shortly afterward helped bring about the open alliance with France that eventually led to British defeat. The **Chew House** (private, NHL) is the most important surviving landmark of the hard fought **Battle of Germantown.**

In an effort to prevent supplies from reaching the British in Philadelphia, the Americans strengthened and reinforced both **Fort Mifflin** (NHL) on the west bank of the Delaware below the city, and **Fort Mercer** on the Jersey shore. A chevaux-de-frise barrier was erected across the river between the two forts. Fort Mercer withstood a British attack on October 22, but Fort Mifflin succumbed to a 6-day siege and fell on the night of November 15–16. This prolonged engagement helped prevent Howe's troops from destroying the American army. The next month Washington went into encampment at Valley Forge. Fort Mifflin, which saw service through World War II, is located on the Delaware River at the foot of Fort Mifflin Road, just east of Philadelphia International Airport, South Philadelphia [1].

No name in American history conveys more of suffering, sacrifice, and triumph than Valley Forge. Eleven thousand ragged, hungry men went into camp here along the Schuylkill River on December 19, 1777. They endured a bitterly cold and harsh winter, but emerged in the spring a trained and disciplined army, a force that could at last meet the enemy on its own terms. Washington selected this site, named for a small iron mill on Valley Creek, because of its defensive position and his ability to watch the approaches to Philadelphia. Approximately 900 log huts were raised and fortifications were thrown up to protect the camp and to command nearby roads and rivers. Throughout the winter the soldiers were rigorously drilled and disciplined by Baron Frederick von Steuben, Washington's drillmaster. When spring came, the army made its debut as a skilled force at the Battle of Monmouth in New Jersey. **Valley Forge State Park** (NHL) embraces 2,000 acres and includes extensive remains of the major forts, lines of earthworks, the artillery park, **Washington's Headquarters** (NHL), **General Frederick William Augustus von Steuben's Headquarters** (NHL), quarters of other top officers, and the grand parade ground. The Mount Joy observation tower affords a comprehensive view of the campsite and the countryside it was designed to command. A dominant feature of the park is the massive **National Memorial Arch** dedicated to the "incomparable patience and fidelity of the soldiery." The Washington Memorial Museum, maintained by the Valley Forge Historical Society, contains hundreds of relics from the encampment, including Washington's field tent. The park is located at Port Kennedy, off the Valley Forge Interchange of the Pennsylvania Turnpike, in Montgomery and Chester Counties [4].

Hopewell Village, near Elverson [5], is one of the oldest ironworks in this country and is a forerunner of today's great iron and steel industry, a dominant factor in the Nation's growth. Hopewell Furnace cast cannon and shot for the American armies during the Amercan Revolution. The village and its industry continued to expand after the war, and, passing through a succession of owners, turned out iron products until new industrial techniques after the Civil War made it obsolete.

**Hopewell Village National Historic Site** is administered by the National Park Service. Interpretation at the site encompasses the furnace operation from 1770 to 1883. Guided tours are provided and during the summer trade and craft demonstration programs are presented in period costume.

Other Pennsylvania sites associated with the Revolution are the **Gates House,** York [6], headquarters for Gen. Horatio Gates while he was president of the Board of War, 1777; **Waynesborough** (private, NHL), Paoli [7], home of Gen. "Mad" Anthony Wayne; **Mount Pleasant** (NHL), Philadelpha [1], onetime home of Benedict Arnold; **Gen. Thaddeus Kosciuszko House,** Philadelphia [1]; and two homes associated with Pennsylvania's signers of the Declaration of Independence: **Summerseat** (private, NHL), Morrisville [8], home of George Clymer; and **George Taylor House** (NHL), Catasaugua [9].

Pennsylvania travel, historic sites, National Park Service, and Bicentennial information can be obtained by writing to:

Bureau of Travel Development, Department of Commerce, South Office Building, Harrisburg, PA 17120

Independence National Historical Park, 313 Walnut St., Philadelphia, PA 19106.

Hopewell Village National Historic Site, R.D. #1, Box 315, Elverson, PA 19520.

Bicentennial Commission of Pennsylvania, William Penn Memorial Museum, Harrisburg, PA 17108.

Rhode Island's resistance to colonial regulations, which foreshadowed the Revolution, began as early as June 1765 with an attack on the British ship "Maidstone" in Newport harbor. In 1769 the British revenue sloop "Liberty" was scuttled, and in June 1772, the "Gaspee" was burned off Warwick. Rhode Island raised 1,500 troops immediately after Lexington, and on May 4, 1776, declared her independence from Great Britain. The colony's total contribution was 4,000 militia and 5,908 army. The only

## Rhode Island

Burning of the *Gaspee*, by C. D. W. Brownell; Rhode Island Historical Society, Providence.

important engagement fought in the State was the Battle of Rhode Island, at Newport, August 29, 1778. It was an inconclusive struggle, but one that prevented the British from advancing farther into the colony from their base at Newport, which they held from December 1776 to October 1779.

Gen. Nathanael Greene, by Charles Willson Peale.

Nathanael Greene Homestead, Coventry.

William Hunter House, Newport.

Vernon House, Newport.

Gaspee Point, Warwick.

A French fleet with 4,000 troops arrived along the Atlantic coast on July 8, 1778. France, who had once been Washington's enemy in the French and Indian War, was now his ally against the British. The French had come to fight, but a series of misunderstandings and poor judgments got things off to a very bad start in the attempts to dislodge the British at Newport. Friction developed early between French admirals and American generals in what appeared to be a well-planned operation, and when a summer storm threatened to damage the fleet, the French simply sailed away to Boston leaving the Americans to fend as best they could—clearly straining allied relations.

The American army was not lost, however, and the ensuing **Battle of Rhode Island,** August 29, 1778, led to the eventual British evacuation of Newport. The site of the first skirmish of this battle, later judged by Lafayette to be the American forces' best fought battle of the war, is marked by a tablet at the intersection of R.I. 138 and Union Street, Portsmouth [1]. The site of the main battle is marked at the intersection of R.I. 114 and 24, Portsmouth [1], by monuments commemorating the "desperate valor" of a regiment of Rhode Island black troops in repelling three "furious assaults" by Hessian regulars.

The **Newport Historic District** [2] (private/public, NHL), bounded approximately by Van Zandt Avenue and Farewell, Sherman, High, Thomas, Golden Hill, Thames, Marsh, and Washington Streets, corresponds roughly to the 18th-century town boundaries. It contains a large number of period buildings and dwellings associated with the Revolution. The District as well as several individual structures has been given National Historic Landmark designation. The structures include the **Old State House** (NHL), used as a hospital for both British and French forces quartered there, the **Vernon House** (private, NHL), headquarters for Count de Rochambeau while the French army occupied Newport, July 1780 to June 1781, the **John Banister House** (private), headquarters for General Prescott during the British occupation, and the **Thomas Robinson House** (private), headquarters of Vicomte de Noailles of the French Army, 1780–81

**Gaspee Point,** off Namquid Drive, Warwick [3], is the site of the seizure and burning of the armed British revenue schooner *Gaspee* by a group of 64 Rhode Island men on the night of June 9, 1772. This very early act of armed resistance to crown authority is commemorated each June by a weeklong celebration in the nearby village of Pawtuxet.

Other Rhode Island sites associated with the Revolution are the **William Hunter House** (NHL), Newport [2], headquarters of Adm. de Terney, commander of the French fleet; **Fort Barton,** Tiverton [4], remaining earthworks of a fort which protected the ferry route across the East Passage of Narragansett Bay; **University Hall** (NHL), Brown University, Providence [5], used as a hospital by the American forces after the Battle of Rhode Island, 1778; **Joseph Brown House** (private), Providence [5], headquarters for Baron de Viomenil during French encampment; **General Nathanael Greene Homestead** (NHL), Coventry [6], the general's home before and during the war; **Governor Stephen Hopkins House** (NHL), Providence [5], home of the Rhode Island signer of the Declaration of Independence; **General James Mitchell Varnum House,** East Greenwich [7], home of the wartime governor of Rhode Island; and the following sites related to the Battle of Rhode Island: **Fort Butts,** Portsmouth [1]; **Green End Fort,** Middletown [8]; and **Tonomy Hill Fort,** Newport [2].

Rhode Island travel, historic sites, and Bicentennial information can be obtained by writing to:

Tourist Promotion Division, Rhode Island Development Council, Roger Williams Building, 49 Hayes St., Providence, RI 02908.

Rhode Island Bicentennial Commission, Roger Williams Building, 49 Hayes St., Providence, RI 02908.

South Carolina was a battleground of rebellion and civil war from 1775 to 1782 and saw more military action than any of the other colonies. A total of 168 separate engagements were fought there, ranging from the British attacks on Charleston to Cherokee incursions on the western border. In no other colony was the struggle between patriot and Tory so pronounced as it was in South Carolina. Twenty thousand State militia served during the war, and the colony gave 6,417 to the Continental Army.

## South Carolina

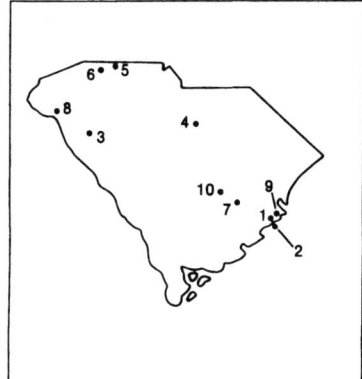

Ferguson Monument, Kings Mountain National Military Park.

Miles Brewton House, Charleston

Gen. Daniel Morgan, by Charles Willson Peale.

Charleston [1] was a besieged and occupied city during the Revolution. As the capital of South Carolina it was the subject of many important events concerning the Southern Campaign. The first British attack came in June of 1776 and was repulsed by William Moultrie's gallant defense on nearby **Sullivan's Island.**

The **Battle of Sullivan's Island,** or **Fort Moultrie** as it came to be called, was one of the most decisive engagements of the American Revolution. Here Col. William Moultrie and about 400 South Carolinians beat off a squadron of 9 British warships on June 28, 1776. This action kept the South free of British control for the next 3 years and allowed southern men and supplies to strengthen the patriot cause in the North.

The present fort was built 1807–11 and was part of the major Civil War military engagements of nearby Fort Sumter. The Revolutionary War fort, no traces of which exist, was considerably different. Military historian Henry B. Carrington, in his *Battles of the American Revolution,* described Fort Moultrie as "laid out for four bastions, . . . the west and north faces of the main work . . . nearly open, and only the two bastions on the channel front . . . sufficiently advanced to receive guns. The soft and spongy but tough palmetto trees which abounded on Sullivan Island, had been dove-tailed together in a series of connecting pens, and these were filled with sand, so that the parapet was 16 feet in thickness, and sufficiently high to protect the gunners and garrison. Thirty-one guns were in position."

The site today is located on Middle Street, Sullivan's Island [2], and is administered by the National Park Service as a part of **Fort Sumter National Monument.** Site interpretation is primarily of the Civil War period.

The British returned 4 years later, captured Charleston, and remained until 1781. Within the two areas that comprise the Charleston Historic District (NHL) are a number of public and private buildings associated with the Revolution. The two areas are bounded by Broad, Bay, Logan, East Battery and South Battery Streets, and by Cumberland, State, Chalmers, and Meeting Streets.

The **Colonial Powder Magazine** was erected in 1703 near the northeast bastion of the city's fortifications on what is now Cumberland Street. This single-story structure of unusually small brick covered with stucco, housed the public powder supply throughout the colonial period until shortly before the fall of Charleston, when the powder was removed and successfully concealed for 2 years in a bricked up portion of the Exchange building on Broad Street. The **Exchange** was constructed in 1767–71 as a customhouse and through the years has served numerous functions. During the Revolution it was the notorious Provost Dungeon where hundreds of Charleston's citizens were imprisoned in cramped vaults for the slightest hint of patriot support. Both the Exchange and Powder House are now museums.

The **Miles Brewton House** (private, NHL), 27 King St., perhaps the most splendid house in Charleston is notable chiefly for its architectural excellence. Built in 1765–69 for a prominent Charleston citizen, the house was commandeered by the British in 1780 as military headquarters for Gen. Sir Henry Clinton.

The five major Revolutionary War engagements in South Carolina were fought at **Ninety-Six, Camden, Kings Mountain, Cowpens,** and **Eutaw Springs.** The village of **Ninety-Six** began as a trading post in 1730 and continued during the colonial period as an important trading center and seat of justice for much of upcountry South Carolina. Its name came from the belief that the town was 96 miles from the frontier post Ft. Prince George, which was actually only about 65 miles away. The village was fortified during the Cherokee outbreak of 1759–60 and was predominantly Tory in sentiment as the Revolution came on. Patriot and Tory forces clashed at Ninety-Six for 3 days in November 1775, but in December the Tories were defeated and dispersed. The British captured Charleston in 1780 and, later in the year, established an outpost and built the Star Fort at Ninety-Six. Gen. Nathanael Greene's American forces invested and assaulted the fort unsuccessfully in May–June 1781 and withdrew as British reinforcements approached. The British ultimately evacuated the fort, however, relinquishing their foothold in upland South Carolina. A stone monument on S.C. 246 stands near the site of the fort and some of the earthworks can still be seen [3].

Five miles north of Camden is the **Camden Battlefield** (NHL) where Gen. Horatio Gates' American army was defeated on August 16, 1780, the worst of a series of disasters to American forces in the South. Though the Americans in this and following engagements with the British were less than victorious, the battle at Camden brought Gen. Nathanael Greene to the fore. A skilled tactical commander second only to Washington, his campaign cleared the southern interior of British troops within a year. Two acres of the Camden Battlefield have been preserved by the D.A.R. just west of U.S. 521 and 601 in Kershaw County [4].

Aroused by the British threat to their homeland, southern Appalachian frontiersmen united and on October 7, 1780, attacked a force of Cornwallis' army and American Tories under Maj. Patrick Ferguson at Kings Mountain, in the foothills of northwestern South Carolina. The success of the frontiersmen at Kings Mountain forced Cornwallis to withdraw from North Carolina, placed him on the defensive, and delayed his northward march for 3 months. It heartened the patriots of the southern colonies and discouraged the Tories in that region. Moreover, it gave the Americans time to create an army under Gen. Nathanael Greene to fight at Cowpens and Guilford Courthouse and thus had a great bearing on the American victory at Yorktown.

The Kings Mountain ridge on which the battle occurred rises from the center of what is now **Kings Mountain National Military Park.** A self-guiding trail leads from the visitor center and museum to the scenes of action on the mountain. The park is located 5 miles from Kings Mountain, N.C. [5], and can be reached from Charlotte, N.C., via Int. 85, from Spartanburg, S.C., via U.S. 29, and from York, S.C., via S.C. 161. Demonstrations of loading and firing the "Brown Bess" and flint-lock "Kentucky" Long Rifle, and Tory camp life in costume are presented throughout the summer.

At a small cattle-grazing area known as the "Cowpens" on January 17, 1781, a force of militia men and Continentals led by Gen. Daniel Morgan defeated British regulars under Lt. Col. Banastre Tarleton. This was a major victory for the American army in the southern theater of operations, for it bolstered their spirits and gave them courage to carry on the fight. The victory also changed British strategy in the South. In an attempt to suppress the main American force under Greene, Cornwallis began a costly march through North Carolina and Virginia that ultimately led to Yorktown.

The fighting at Cowpens took place over a distance of about 600 yards southeast of the intersection of present-day S.C. 11 and 110 (northwest of Int. 85) [6]. Only a portion of the original battlefield has been preserved. A commemorative monument erected by the Federal Government stands near what was the American lines in the angle of the highway intersection. **Cowpens National Battlefield** is adminstered by the National Park Service through Kings Mountain National Military Park, where visitor center exhibits interpret the military action.

**Eutaw Springs** was the last major engagement of the Revolution in South Carolina. Here, on September 8, 1781, General

Greene's Continentals shattered Col. Archibald Stuart's British command. This led to the British evacuation of Orangeburg, leaving the Americans in undisputed possession of the interior of South Carolina. The **Eutaw Battlefield,** 3 miles east of Eutawville on S.C. 6, is now a State park [7].

Other South Carolina sites associated with the Revolution are **Hopewell** (private), near Pendleton [8], home of Gen. Andrew Pickens; **Gov. John Rutledge House** (private), Charleston [1], home of the wartime governor; **Snee Farm** (private), near Mt. Pleasant [9], home of Charles Pinckney; **Drayton Hall,** 12 miles from Charleston [1], home of political leader William Drayton; **Fort Dorchester State Park,** near Charleston [1]; **Col. William Washington House** (private), Charleston [1]; **Col. John Stuart House** (private), Charleston [1]; **Fort Camden,** Camden [4]; **Fort Johnson Powder Magazine,** James Island, Charleston Harbor [1]; and the homes of the colony's four signers of the Declaration of Independence: **Hopsewee-on-the-Santee** (NHL), Santee [10], home of Thomas Lynch, Jr.; **Middleton Place** (house is private, grounds open to public; NHL), 13 miles from Charleston [1], home of Arthur Middleton; **Edward Rutledge House** (private, NHL), Charleston [1]; and **Heyward-Washington House,** Charleston [1], home of Thomas Heyward.

South Carolina travel, historic sites, National Park Service, and Bicentennial information can be obtained by writing to·

South Carolina Department of Parks, Recreation and Tourism, P.O. Box 1358, Columbia, SC 29202.

Fort Moultrie, c/o Fort Sumter National Monument, P.O. Box 428, Sullivan's Island, SC 29482

Kings Mountain National Military Park and Cowpens National Battlefield, P O. Box 31, Kings Mountain, NC 28086

South Carolina American Revolution Bicentennial Commission, P.O Box 1358, Columbia, SC 29202.

The Vermont wilderness had barely been explored at the outbreak of the Revolution, and the area was not a colony. Throughout the Revolutionary years it was known as the New Hampshire Grants and was the subject of controversy between New York and New Hampshire. The State did not gain independent status until 1791. The Battle of Hubbardton, during Burgoyne's 1777 campaign, was the only major military action in Vermont.

## Vermont

 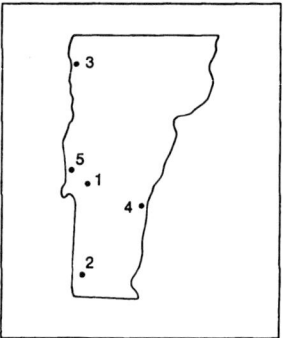

Bennington Battle Monument, Bennington.

Ethan Allen, Statuary Hall, U.S. Capitol, Washington, D.C.

Colonels Seth Warner and Ebenezer Francis, commanding the rearguard of the retreating American force after the fall of Fort Ticonderoga in July 1777, remained overnight at Hubbardton without taking proper security measures for their encampment. A detachment of General Burgoyne's British forces attacked the next morning, July 7, precipitating a short but very severe fight. The Americans scattered with instructions to reassemble at Manchester. Francis was killed. The British advance was delayed, but the cost was high. The **Hubbardton Battlefield** [1] is now a 50-acre State park.

Other Vermont sites associated with the Revolution are **Bennington Battle Monument,** Bennington [2] (see New York for **Bennington Battlefield**); **Ethan Allen Grave and Monument,** Burlington [3]; the **Old Constitution House,** Windsor [4], where Vermont's constitution was written and adopted; and **Mount Independence** (NHL), Addison County [5], major American fortress and part of the Fort Ticonderoga military complex.

Vermont travel, historic sites, and Bicentennial information can be obtained by writing to:

Information and Travel Division, Vermont Agency of Development and Community Affairs, 63 Elm St., Montpelier, VT 05602.

Vermont Bicentennial Commission, Office of the Lieutenant Governor, Montpelier, VT 05602.

While Virginia immediately and wholeheartedly supported Massachusetts in denouncing the Intolerable Acts that brought on the Revolution, the Old Dominion was more directly interested in the Quebec Act which threatened to cut off western territories that she claimed. Like Massachusetts, Virginia's patriots were outspoken in their opposition to Parliament's colonial policy. Washington, Jefferson, Patrick Henry, George Rogers Clark, all served the patriot cause in one way or another throughout the

## Virginia

Fifers and drummers of the Colonial Williamsburg Militia Company performing on Market Square Green, Williamsburg.

Gen. Henry "Lighthorse Harry" Lee, a sketch from the Gilbert Stuart portrait, by Benson J. Lossing.

Revolutionary years. In October 1775 hostilities broke out between patriot and Loyalist forces when Governor Lord Dunmore captured and burned Norfolk. The British did not descend on Virginia in force until the closing year of the war. Thirty thousand Virginia men served in the militia, while 26,678 served under Washington's command.

Thomas Jefferson, by Charles Willson Peale.

Monticello, Charlottesville.

Interior of Wakefield, George Washington Birthplace National Monument.

Surrender Room, Moore House, Yorktown Battlefield.

Wakefield, George Washington Birthplace National Monument.

Stratford Hall, Lerty.

Mount Vernon.

Gunston Hall, near Lorton.

Victory Monument, Yorktown Battlefield

The Storming of Redoubt No. 10, by Louis Eugene Lami; State Capitol, Richmond.

Moore House, Yorktown Battlefield.

Redoubt No. 9, Yorktown Battlefield.

Lord Cornwallis, from an early engraving.

The Surrender of Cornwallis at Yorktown, from an early engraving.

Williamsburg [1] was the capital of Virginia from 1699 to 1780 and was most important as a political and cultural center. Patrick Henry, Thomas Jefferson, George Washington, George Mason, George Wythe, Edmund Randolph, and other leading patriots served as burgesses here. They debated and resolved the issues that resulted in many of our democratic concepts, and played major roles in the movement for independence. Today 500 restored and reconstructed buildings make up the 130 acres of **Colonial Williamsburg, Inc.,** a corporation founded and financed by the late John D. Rockefeller, Jr. Painstaking research and planning has recreated the Colonial capital much as it was at the height of the Revolutionary movement. The most notable reconstructions are the **Capitol,** rebuilt to the exact specifications of the original, the **Governor's Palace,** and **Raleigh Tavern,** where many Revolutionary activities were planned. The Williamsburg Historic District is a National Historic Landmark.

As the principal seaport and commercial center for northern Virginia during the American Revolution, **Alexandria** [2] witnessed many dramatic events. George Washington and George Mason lived nearby and had important connections in the city. The **Alexandria Historic District** (NHL), bounded approximately by the Capital Beltway, Alfred, Patrick, Oronoco, and Princess Streets, the George Washington Memorial Parkway, and the Potomac River, includes a number of public and private buildings dating from the Revolution. One of the most notable of these is Gadsby's Tavern (NHL), 128 North Royal St., which, like Raleigh Tavern in Williamsburg, was a favorite meeting place for political leaders.

Near Alexandria are two important homes associated with Revolutionary personalities. Seven miles south is **Mount Vernon** (NHL) [3], home and burial site of George Washington. The Mount Vernon mansion was built in 1743. Washington inherited the 8,000-acre estate in 1752, and it remained his home until his death in 1799. Although the house has no direct association with the war, a number of the general's personal military possessions are displayed in the several buildings. The Mount Vernon Ladies Association rescued the 500-acre Mansion House Farm from near destruction in 1858.

A few miles further south in Fairfax County is **Gunston Hall** (NHL) [4], the home of George Mason, a major Virginia political leader during and after the Revolution. Among his more notable writings were the Fairfax Resolves of 1774, defining the constitutional relationship of the American Colonies to England, and the Virginia Declaration of Rights in 1776, which influenced the Declaration of Independence.

Two miles south of Charlottesville [5], in Albemarle County, is **Monticello** (NHL), the home of Thomas Jefferson, author of the Declaration of Independence, member of the Continental Congress, wartime governor of Virginia and third President of the United States. The house and gardens are owned by the Thomas Jefferson Memorial Foundation.

**Stratford Hall** (NHL), 3 miles north of Lerty in Westmoreland County [6], has been referred to as the birthplace of revolutionary leaders. Built by Col. Thomas Lee in 1725–30, it was the home of Richard Henry Lee and Francis Lightfoot Lee, both signers of the Declaration of Independence. In 1807 this massive brick mansion was the birthplace of Robert E. Lee. Today it is owned by the Robert E. Lee Memorial Foundation.

**Wakefield** [7], 38 miles east of Fredericksburg, was the birthplace and boyhood home of George Washington. Time had leveled virtually all building remains at the plantation site when in 1931–32 the War Department and the Wakefield Association reconstructed a memorial house over one of the foundations uncovered in 1896. The site today is administered by the National Park Service as the **George Washington Birthplace National Monument** and serves as an illustration of early 18th-century life. Guided tours are provided through the house and "Living Farm" demonstrations are presented on the plantation.

On March 23, 1775, just a few weeks before the clash of arms at Lexington and Concord, Patrick Henry, member of the Virginia House of Burgesses, made his "Give me liberty, or give me death" speech that sounded the call to arms for Virginians and all Americans. He delivered the speech at a meeting of the general assembly in **St. John's Episcopal Church** (NHL), Richmond [8]. Although altered somewhat since first built in 1740, the church still stands on East Broad Street between 24th and 25th Streets.

At Yorktown, on October 19, 1781, Lord Cornwallis surrendered his British army to a besieging American and French force commanded by Gen. George Washington. This set in motion events which brought England to the peace table and a subsequent recognition of this country as an independent nation.

The campaign ended in a classic military siege of the fortified port of Yorktown in which the allied American and French forces encircled the British fortifications at Yorktown and Gloucester

Point across the York River. They then erected their first siege line against Yorktown. As the British weakened under continuous artillery fire the Allies erected an even closer siege line. Lord Cornwallis, despairing of relief, surrendered his force rather than waste his men's lives.

The end was sheer pageantry. The British army in bright uniforms marched out between contrasting lines of ragged Continentals and elegantry uniformed French troops. Their colors cased and marching to a doleful tune on drums and fifes, the British were surrendered to Gen. Benjamin Lincoln who ordered the column to a field where they laid down their arms.

Although formal peace was 2 years away, Yorktown proved the conclusive military event of the Revolution.

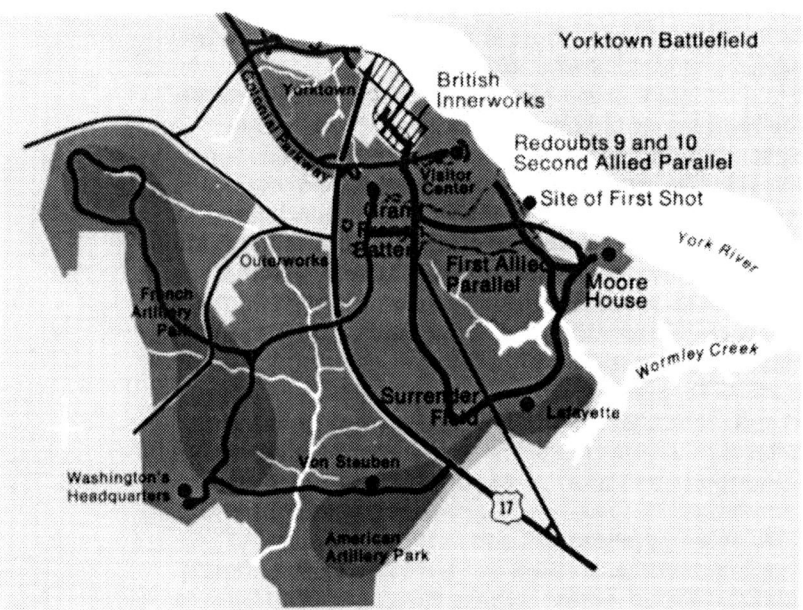

Today a self-guiding motor tour road links Yorktown with its historic structures, the fortifications and encampment areas of both armies, the Moore House where the articles of capitulation were negotiated, and Surrender Field. The park also includes the home of Thomas Nelson, Jr., Continental officer, wartime governor, and signer of the Declaration of Independence.

A visitor center provides information and orientation to the visitor concerning the events leading up to the battle.

**Yorktown Battlefield** lies in and around the village of Yorktown [9] on the peninsula between the York and James Rivers, and is linked with Jamestown, scene of the first successful English settlement in America, by the Colonial Parkway. All three units are administered as **Colonial National Historical Park.** With nearby Colonial Williamsburg, the park offers a vivid panorama of America's colonial and Revolutionary War history.

Other Virginia sites associated with the Revolution are **Grace Church,** Yorktown [9], used as a powder magazine during the British occupation; **Saratoga** (private), Boyce [10], home of Gen. Daniel Morgan, built by Hessian prisoners; **Lansdowne** (private), Urbanna [11], home of the younger brother of Francis Lightfoot, Richard Henry, and Henry (Lighthorse Harry) Lee, and controversial diplomat Arthur Lee; **Gen. Hugh Mercer Apothecary Shop,** Fredericksburg [12]; **Sentry Box** (private), home of Gen. George Weedon, Fredericksburg [12]; **Hanover Court House and Tavern,** Hanover [13]; **Scotchtown** (NHL), Ashland [14], home of Patrick Henry; **Peyton Randolph House** (NHL), Williamsburg [1], home of the President of the Continental Congress, 1774–75; and four additional homes associated with Virginia's signers of the Declaration of Independence: **Berkeley** (NHL), Charles City County [15], home of Benjamin Harrison; **Elsing Green** (private, NHL), King William Courthouse [16], home of Carter Braxton; **Menokin** (private, NHL), Warsaw [17], home of Francis Lightfoot Lee; and **George Wythe House** (NHL), Williamsburg [1].

Virginia travel, historic sites, National Park Service, and Bicentennial information can be obtained by writing to.

Virginia State Travel Service, 911 East Broad St., Richmond, VA 23219.

George Washington Birthplace National Monument, c/o Fredericksburg and Spotsylvania County Battlefields Memorial National Military Park, P.O. Box 679, Fredericksburg, VA 22401.

Colonial National Historical Park, P O Box 210, Yorktown, VA 23490.

Virginia Independence Bicentennial Commission, Drawer JF, Williamsburg, VA 23185.

What is now West Virginia was a part of the Virginia colony during the Revolution. Though many men from this area fought in the war and several Continental Army officers made their homes here, there were no military campaigns in these western counties.

## West Virginia

Gen. Adam Stephen House, Martinsburg.

Traveller's Rest, home of Gen. Horatio Gates, Leetown.

Spinning wheel, Gen. Adam Stephen House, Martinsburg.

Gen. Horatio Gates, by Charles Willson Peale.

Three historic sites in West Virginia are associated with the Revolution: **Traveller's Rest** (private, NHL), Leetown [1], home of Gen. Horatio Gates, 1773–90; **Pratio Rio** (private), Leetown [1], home of Gen. Charles Lee; and **General Adam Stephen House,** Martinsburg [2].

West Virginia travel, historic sites, and Bicentennial information can be obtained by writing to:

Department of Commerce, Travel Development Division, 1900 Washington St. E, Charleston, WV 25305.

West Virginia American Revolution Bicentennial Commission, State Office Building #6, Room B-531, 1900 Washington St. E, Charleston, WV 25305.

While American forces were defending the colonies along the Atlantic seaboard, the western frontiers, from New York and Pennsylvania to what is now Kentucky and Tennessee, were being savagely assaulted by Indians under British officers. Fortunately for the Americans, the frontier settlements held firm. The Indian threat was met in the southern areas in the Battle of Long Island Flats in 1776, and in one of the last actions of the Revolution at the Battle of Blue Licks, 1782.

## The Western Frontier

Gathering of the Mountain Men, by Lloyd Branson; Tennessee State Archives.

Lt. Col. Henry Hamilton, British governor of Detroit and defender of Fort Sackville; Harvard University Portrait Collection

Clark leads his men across the Wabash

Fort Sackville surrendered, from murals at George Rogers Clark National Historical Park, Vincennes, Ind.

Reconstructed Fort Harrod, Pioneer Memorial State Park, Harrodsburg, Ky.

Statue of George Rogers Clark, George Rogers Clark National Historical Park, Vincennes, Ind.

George Rogers Clark, copy of an original by J. W. Jarvis; Executive Mansion, Richmond. Va.

Long Island of the Holston (private, NHL) is an island approximately 4 miles long and ½ mile wide in the South Fork of the Holston River at Kingsport, Tenn. [1]. The eastern section of the island is developed today, but the western portion looks very much as it did in July 1776 when the Cherokees attacked a pioneer settlement there in what has become known as the **Battle of Long Island Flats.** The defeat of the Indians and a subsequent American expedition against Indian villages brought a 2-year peace to the southwestern frontier. It was from Long Island on March 10, 1775, that Daniel Boone, with 30 axemen, began the task of marking the famous Wilderness Road that opened Kentucky to white settlement.

The administrative center for the first settlements in what is now Tennessee was located on **Sycamore Shoals** (private, NHL), two miles west of Elizabethton [2], on the Watauga River. **Fort Watauga** was erected in 1775 after the purchase of the land from the Cherokees. The Indians attacked the fort unsuccessfully in 1776. The site has long since been lost but is believed to be on a low ridge beside Tenn. 67, about one-half mile southwest of the lower end of Sycamore Shoals. A stone marker is located nearby, surrounded by a residential development. It was from this point in 1780 that the Tennessee Mountain Men marched to Kings Mountain in South Carolina.

A State park of 100 acres along U.S. 68 near **Blue Lick Springs** [3] commemorates the Battle of Blue Licks, often called the "last battle of the Revolution." On August 19, 1782, Indians ambushed and defeated a pursuing force of Kentuckians under Daniel Boone in the worst defeat suffered by an American force in Kentucky during the Revolution.

Two very important forts were constructed in what is now Kentucky during the early years of the Revolution: **Fort Boonesborough** in 1775 by Daniel Boone, and **Fort Harrod** in 1777 by James Harrod. Indians repeatedly attacked and besieged both during the war, but the forts survived to become the focal points for large communities. Nothing remains of Fort Boonesborough, but the Daughters of the American Revolution has placed a marker at the site 9 miles north of Richmond [4] on U.S. 227. Fort Harrod has been partially reconstructed and is a part of **Pioneer Memorial State Park,** Lexington and Warwick Streets, Harrodsburg [5]. It was while at Fort Harrod that George Rogers Clark planned his campaign of 1778–79 that led to the conquest of the Old Northwest Territory.

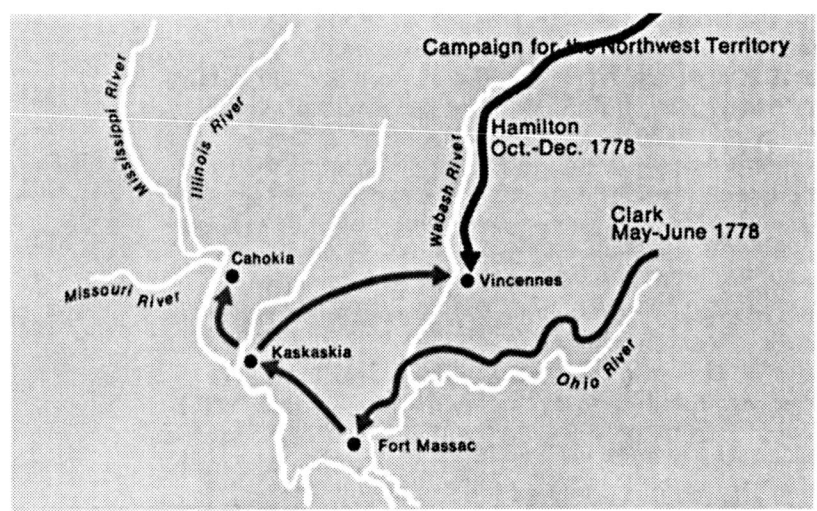

Another Kentucky site associated with the Revolution is **Locust Grove,** Louisville [6], George Rogers Clark's home in the later years of his life.

During the Revolution, the British exerted every effort to keep the Thirteen Original Colonies from extending control into the Old Northwest Territory. As a part of their strategy, they incited their Indian allies to raid Pennsylvania, New York, and Virginia frontier settlements. George Rogers Clark, a surveyor turned soldier and the commander of the Kentucky militia, conceived the daring plan of attacking British posts to win the Northwest Territory for Virginia and to halt the Indian attacks. In July 1778, acting under orders from Gov. Patrick Henry of Virginia, Clark and a force of about 150 men captured the French outpost-trading centers of Kaskaskia, Cahokia, and Vincennes in the Illinois country.

In short order the British sent Lt. Gov. Henry Hamilton from Detroit to retake Vincennes and Fort Sackville which defended it. This was accomplished on December 17, 1778. When Clark learned about it, he moved swiftly. With about 170 men, he left Kaskaskia in February 1779 and marched on Vincennes. After a journey beset by many hardships, the little band surprised the British garrison, and on February 25, 1779, Hamilton surrendered. Clark's military dominance over the Northwest Territory throughout the remainder of the war was a prime factor in causing the

British to cede the region to the United States in the 1783 peace treaty.

The **George Rogers Clark National Historical Park,** Vincennes, Ind. [7], with its memorial on the site of Fort Sackville, commemorates the winning of the Old Northwest Territory and the achievements of Clark and his men on the western frontier in the American Revolution. The park is located off Vigo Street, near the Lincoln Memorial Bridge, in Vincennes. The memorial building contains a statue of George Rogers Clark and a series of paintings depicting the events leading to the winning of the Old Northwest. Although the building is inaccessible to wheelchairs, year-round costumed demonstrations of loading and firing the flint-lock "Kentucky" Long Rifle are available to everyone.

Travel, historic sites, National Park, and Bicentennial information for Indiana, Tennessee, and Kentucky can be obtained by writing to:

Division of Tourism, Indiana Department of Commerce, State House, Indianapolis, IN 46204.

George Rogers Clark National Historical Park, 115 Dubois St., Vincennes, IN 47591.

Indiana American Revolution Bicentennial Commission, 504 State Office Building, Indianapolis, IN 46204.

Travel, Frankfort, KY 40601.

Kentucky Historical Events Celebration Commission, Room 1005, Capital Plaza Office Tower, Frankfort, KY 40601.

Division of Information and Tourist Promotion, Tennessee Department of Conservation, 2611 West End Ave., Nashville, TN 37203.

State Historical Society, Historical Building, Nashville, TN 37219.

# A CHRONOLOGY OF POLITICAL AND MILITARY EVENTS OF THE AMERICAN REVOLUTION

|   1763   |   1764   |   1765   |

**February 10**
Treaty of Paris ends
French and Indian War.

**March 22**
Stamp Act tax imposed by
Parliament.

**April 5**
Sugar Act replaces
Molasses Act of 1733.

**May 24**
James Otis speaks out
against "taxation without
representation."

**May 29**
Patrick Henry proposes
Virginia Resolutions.

**June 12**
Massachusetts forms Committee of Correspondence.

**October 7**
Proclamation of 1763 signed
by George III.

**October 9–25**
Stamp Act Congress, New
York City

1766 | 1767 | 1768

March 18
Parliament repeals Stamp Act.

June 29
Townshend Acts imposed on colonies.

October 1
Two regiments of British troops arrive in Boston, Mass.

|  1769  |  1770  |

**May 16**
Virginia Resolves condemn Parliament for tax and other policies.

**May 18**
Virginia Association formed; nonimportation agreement established; followed soon by other colonies.

**March 5**
Boston "Massacre."

**April 12**
Townshend Acts repealed, except tea duty.

                1771                    1772                    1773

May 16
Uprising of "Regulators"
climaxes in Battle of
Alamance Creek in North
Carolina.

June 9
British customs schooner
*Gaspee* attacked off coast
of Providence, R.I.

December 16
"Boston Tea Party."

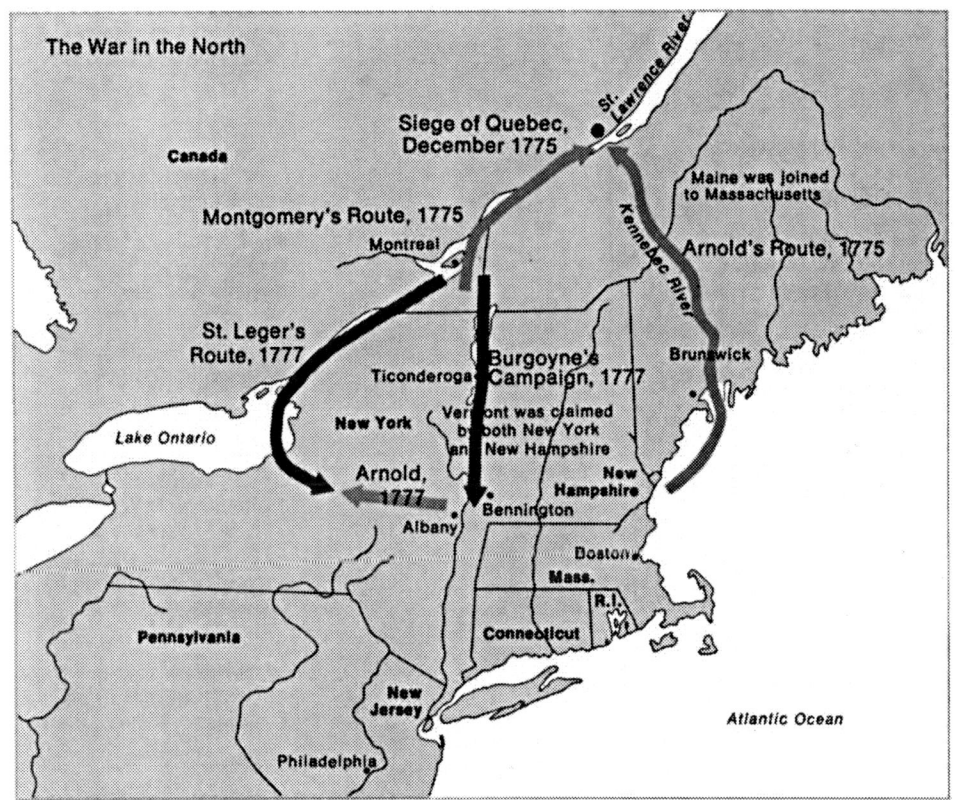

## 1774

**March 31**
Boston Port Bill, first of Coercive ("Intolerable") Acts closes Boston harbor.

**May 30**
Quebec Act extends Canadian boundary south to Ohio River.

**June 2**
New Quartering Act extends billeting of British troops to private dwellings.

**September 5**
First Continental Congress convenes in Philadelphia, Pa.

**October 14**
"Declaration and Resolves" of Congress condemns most British acts since 1763.

**October 26**
Congress adjourns.

**December 14**
Fort William and Mary (later Fort Constitution), Portsmouth, N.H., raided by patriots.

**January**
Population of colonies estimated at 2,600,000.

**March 23**
Patrick Henry's "Liberty or Death" speech before Virginia Assembly.

**April 6**
Boone founds Boonesborough in Kentucky.

**May 10**
Ethan Allen and Benedict Arnold take Fort Ticonderga, N.Y.

**June 12**
British schooner *Margaretta* taken by patriots at Machias, Maine.

**July 3**
Washington takes command of Continental Army at Cambridge, Mass.

**September 2**
Washington commissions first naval squadron of schooners.

**October 13**
Continental navy and marines authorized.

**November 5**
Hopkins appointed commander in chief of American naval fleet.

**December 8–31**
Siege of Quebec.

## 1775

April 19
Battles at Lexington and Concord, Mass.

April 20
Siege of Boston begins.

May 10
Second Continental Congress convenes at Philadelphia, Pa.

May 12
British Crown Point, N.Y., falls to the Americans

May 16
Arnold takes St. John's in Canada.

June 15
George Washington appointed commander in chief of Continental Army.

June 17
Battle at Bunker Hill (Breeds Hill), Charlestown, Mass.

September 7
American *Hannah* takes British *Unity*—first capture by a Continental vessel

September 24
Benedict Arnold begins march on Quebec from Ft. Western, Augusta, Maine.

November 9
George III declares colonies in open state of rebellion.

November 10
United States Marine Corps established

November 19
Battle at Ninety-Six, S.C.

December 11
Royal Gov. Dunmore of Virginia defeated by patriots at Norfolk.

December 23
Royal proclamation closes colonies to all trade as of March 7, 1776.

December 31
Arnold's attack on Quebec fails; Montgomery killed.

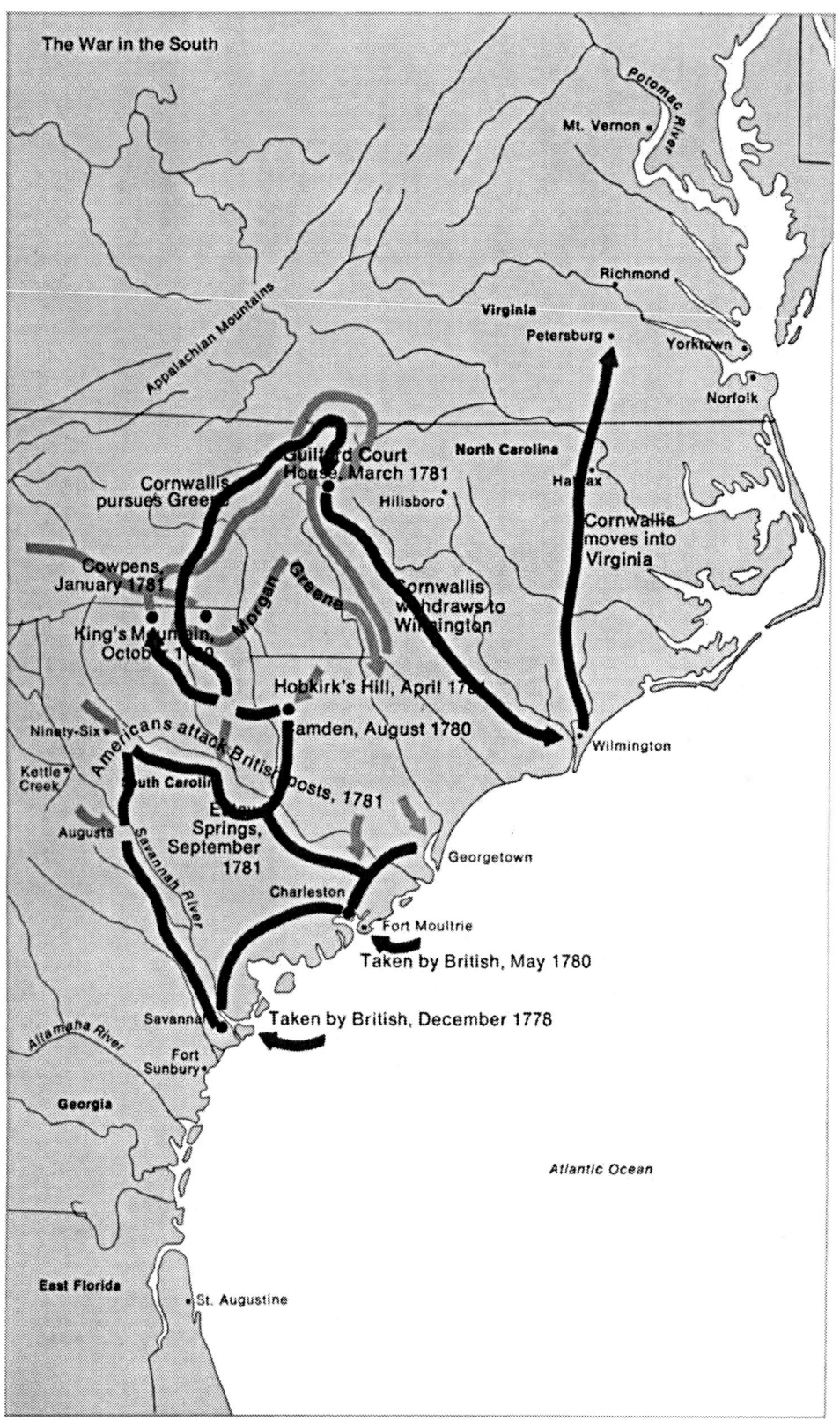

1776

January 10
Thomas Paine publishes pamphlet *Common Sense*.

February 27
Battle at Moores Creek, N.C.

March 17
Siege of Boston ends; British evacuate city; *Alfred-Glasgow* encounter, off Block Island, N.Y.

June 7
*Yankee Hero-Melford* engagement, near Boston.

June 28
Thomas Jefferson presents Declaration of Independence to Congress.

June 28
Battle of Sullivan's Island, S.C.

July 4
John Hancock first to sign the Declaration of Independence at Philadelphia

August 26–27
Battle of Long Island (Brooklyn), N.Y.

September 11
Peace conference at Conference House, Staten Island, N.Y., fails.

September 15
New York City occupied by British.

September 16
Battle at Harlem Heights, N.Y.C.

October 11–13
Battle at Valcour Bay, N.Y.

October 18
British naval forces burn Falmouth, Maine.

October 28
Battle at White Plains, N.Y.

November 16
Fort Washington, N.Y., surrendered to British.

November 18
Fort Lee, N.J., surrendered.

November 18–December 20
Washington's retreat across New Jersey into Pennsylvania.

December 8
British occupy Newport, R.I.

December 25
Washington crosses Delaware River into New Jersey.

December 26
Battle of Trenton, N.J.

1777

January 3
Battle of Princeton, N.J.

January 6–May 28
Winter encampment at
Morristown, N.J.

January 29
British occupy Augusta, Ga.

May 17
Battle of Thomas Creek,
Fla.

June 17
Gen. John Burgoyne begins
campaign to isolate
New England.

July 5
Americans evacuate
Fort Ticonderoga.

July 6
Crown Point, N.Y.,
evacuated by American
troops.

July 7
Battle at Hubbardton, Vt.

August 2–22
Siege of Fort Stanwix, N.Y.

August 6
Battle at Oriskany, N.Y.

August 16
Battle of Bennington in
New York.

September 3
Battle at Cooch's Bridge,
New Castle County, Del.

September 11
Battle of Brandywine, Pa.

September 19
Battle of Freeman Farm
(Saratoga), N.Y.

October 4
Battle at Germantown, Pa.

October 6
British take Fort Mont-
gomery and Fort Clinton,
N.Y.

October 7
Battle at Bemis Heights
(Saratoga), N.Y.

November 10–15
Siege of Fort Mifflin, Pa.

December 17
France recognizes
independence of
United States.

December 19
Winter encampment at
Valley Forge, Pa., begins.

September 26
British occupy Philadelphia.

October 17
Burgoyne surrenders at
Saratoga.

October 22
Battle of Red Bank
(Fort Mercer), N.J.

1778

February 6
Franco-American Alliance
concluded (ratified by
Congress on May 4).

April 14–May 8
Capt. John Paul Jones in
*Ranger* invades Irish Sea;
takes a British fort and a
British sloop-of-war.

May 6
British naval expedition
into Delaware Bay destroys
44 American vessels.

June 18
British evacuate
Philadelphia.

June 19
American army leaves
Valley Forge in pursuit of
British.

June 28
Battle of Monmouth, N.J.
Battle of Fort Sullivan
(Moultrie), S.C.

July 8
French troops arrive off
coast of Rhode Island.

August 29
Battle of Rhode Island,
Newport, R.I.

November 11
Cherry Valley Massacre,
N.Y.

December 29
Savannah, Ga., taken by
British.

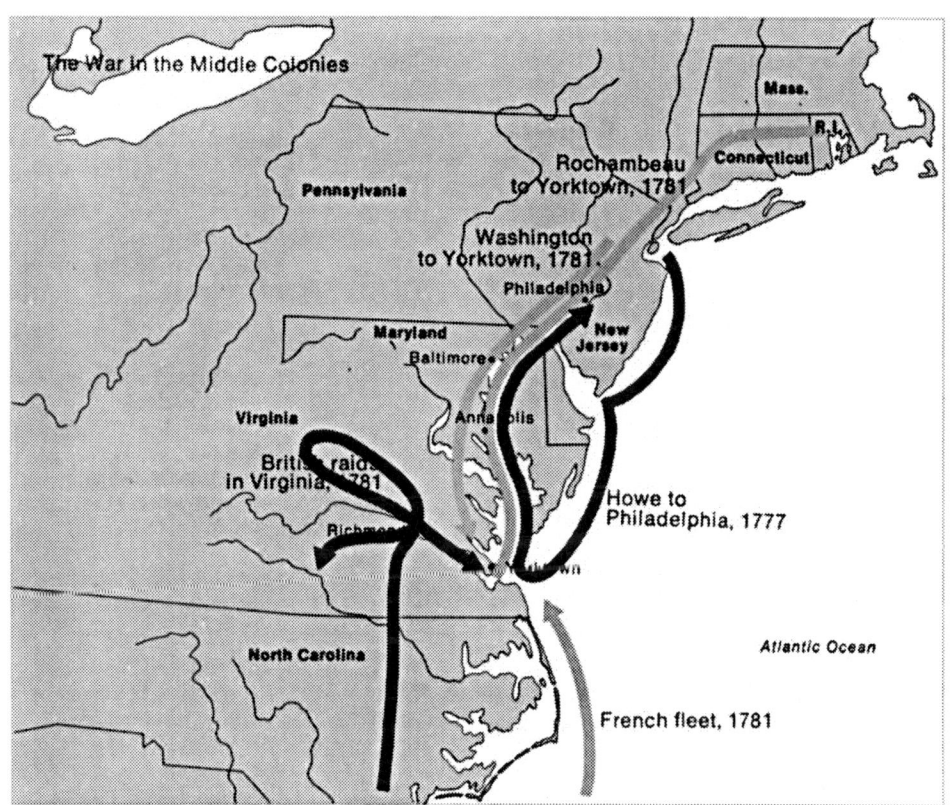

1779

February 14
Battle of Kettle Creek, Ga.

February 24
Battle of Fort Sackville,
Vincennes, Ind.

March 29
British siege of Charleston,
S.C. begins.

May 5
Mutiny breaks out in
American camp at
Morristown, N.J.

June 2
*Trumbull-Watt* engagement,
north of Bermuda.

July 15–16
Battle of Stony Point, N.Y.

July 19–22
Battle at Minisink, N.Y.

August 29–September 15
Sullivan and Clinton expedition against Indians
in northwestern New York.

August 29
Battle of Newtown, N.Y.

August 3
Benedict Arnold placed in
charge of fortifications at
West Point, N.Y.

September 3–October 26
Siege of Savannah, Ga.

September 23
*Bonhomme Richard-Serapis*
engagement, in North Sea
off York, England.

September 23
Arnold's intermediary with
British, Major John André,
captured.

October 2
André executed.

December 1, 1779–June 22, 1780
Winter encampment at
Morristown. N.J.

1780

May 12
Charleston surrendered
to British.

June 9
*Protector-Duff* engagement,
off Newfoundland.

August 16
Battle of Camden, S.C.

September 25
Arnold flees to the British
side.

October 7
Battle of Kings Mountain,
S.C.

October 17
Attack on Old Stone Fort,
Schoharie, N.Y.

October 19
Battle of Klock's Field, N.Y.

## 1781

**January 1**
2,400 Pennsylvania troops mutiny over non-pay.

**January 7**
Mutiny ends but 1,200 men leave army.

**January 17**
Battle of Cowpens, S.C.

**March 15**
Battle of Guilford Courthouse, N.C.

**May 9**
Fort George, Pensacola, Fla., surrendered to Spanish.

**May 22**
Washington and Rochambeau meet in Wethersfield, Conn., to plan French-American military campaign.

**May 22–June 19**
Siege of Ninety-Six, S.C.

**May 22–June 6**
Siege of Augusta, Ga.

**August 8**
*Trumbull-Iris* engagement, off Halifax.

**August 30**
French fleet arrives off Yorktown, Virginia.

**September 5–10**
British naval attack on French fleet in Chesapeake Bay at Yorktown fails

**September 6**
Arnold–British attack on Fort Griswold, New London, Conn.
*Congress-Savage* engagement, off Charleston, S.C.

**September 8**
Battle of Eutaw Springs, S.C.

**September 28–October 19**
Siege of Yorktown.

**October 19**
British surrender at Yorktown.